Walk on the Wild Side

LOU REED

Lou Reed: Walk on the Wild Side: The Stories
Behind the Songs
Copyright © 2004 by Carlton Books
All rights reserved

Published by Hal Leonard Corporation
7777 Bluemound Road
P.O. Box 13819
Milwaukee, WI 53213

Trade Book Division Editorial Offices
151 West 46th Street, 8th Floor
New York, NY 10036

Published in Great Britain by Carlton Books Limited
20 Mortimer Street
London W1T 3JW

Library of Congress Cataloging-in-Publication Data

Roberts, Chris.
Lou Reed : walk on the wild side : the stories behind
the songs /
by Chris Roberts.-- 1st ed.
p. cm.
Includes bibliographical references.
Discography: p.
ISBN 0-634-08032-6

1. Reed, Lou. 2. Rock musicians--United States--
Biography. I. Title.
ML420.R299R62 2004
782.42166'092--dc22
2004012497

Visit Hal Leonard online at www.halleonard.com

Project editor: Lorna Russell
Picture research: Sarah Edwards
Art Editor: Vicky Holmes
Cover design: Karin Fremer
Production: Lisa Moore

LOU REED (CENTER) AS AN UNDERGRADUATE PERFORMING AT SYRACUSE UNIVERSITY, CA. 1963. GERARD MALANGA COLLECTION.

Walk on the Wild Side

LOU REED

The Stories Behind the Songs Chris Roberts

HAL•LEONARD®

ANDY WARHOL WITH THE VELVET UNDERGROUND & NICO, HOLLYWOOD - 1966. PHOTO © GERARD MALANGA.

CONTENTS

AN INTERVIEW WITH LOU REED

Lou Reed was once The Man, which, whatever he is now, is once more than most of us. For a crucial time the epitome of adventurous, literate, sexually challenging rock'n'roll, Lou, 62 on 2 March 2004, is a hi-fi buff who sells spectacles – "Lou's Views" – on his website. He also makes meditation music – "good for doing the various Chi's" – and publishes big books of his photography. A post-Velvet Underground career of close to thirty solo albums began sensationally in the '70s with glamorous, emotional swaggers-for-help like the Bowie-produced *Transformer*, the marvellously depressing *Berlin* and the sleazy-but-nice *Coney Island Baby*. In this period, he was a junkie-poet demigod, contrary and inspired. A role model for misfits who don't admit to having role models. Labelled "the godfather of punk" (one of them, anyway) with the graphic *Street Hassle*, he underperformed through the next decade, married to his manager and becoming a mullet-haired blouson-wearing self-parody. 1989's *New York* brought him back to critical favour: since then, worthy, intelligent, crushingly dull albums about Warhol and death have done well. A "Satellite Of Love" remix recently swept dance floors.

Perhaps we've undersold the fact he was the broken-glass voice and tangled sinful heart of the Velvet Underground, the most influential band of all time, apart, obviously, from the Bee Gees ...? Lou has always either denied or invoked the importance of the Velvets, usually depending on that day's fragility of his ego and ever-mercurial moods.

He has around now a new double live album out, called *Animal Serenade*. It documents Reed and his musicians playing in LA last year. They rework such anthems as "Venus In Furs", "Heroin" and "All Tomorrow's Parties", strip down three songs from the doomed masterpiece *Berlin*, and pick over more recent material. At one point Lou proves that "Sweet Jane" is four chords, not three: this matters to him. Later on the opus, he compares his writing to that of Burroughs, Algren and Tennessee Williams. Lou is notoriously snippy with journalists, usually scaring them. Long ago he studied journalism (and literature) himself.

Today, Lou (who's been the partner of art-house musician Laurie Anderson for years) is relatively accommodating, although the innate sarcasm kicks in when I ask if the one-time bisexual speed freak is a clean-living man these days. "Oh no, I'm worse than ever," he deadpans. Reed invented "deadpan". "I'm smoking a fucking crack pipe as we speak, can't you tell? C'mon. I'm the only vegan crackhead in New York." It's not going to be easy to get him to talk about his gloriously debauched past, either. "Why would I go and listen to my old albums? That would be

like jerking off. Do you read stuff you wrote years ago? No, right? You do something new. I'd rather listen to something new by somebody else that I've never heard before."

Such as?

"All kinds of things. Some of the hip-hop stuff that's out sounds great. Just the sound – forget what they're saying, forget that. The production's amazing. Like OutKast's 'Hey Ya' – put that on headphones, and holy shit! What's going on in there is unbelievable. It's so smart, God, it's perfect pop. You hear that and you feel good."

Is "Sweet Jane" perfect pop?

"Well, I maintain it's that fourth chord, that little hop at the end, that makes that song what it is, makes it fly. Otherwise you've got 'Twist And Shout'."

Are you sure I can't push you down Memory Lane?

"Follow the dotted line. Look, put all the songs together and it's certainly an autobiography. It's just not necessarily mine. I write about other people, tell stories, always did. I've had no more or less high spots and low spots than anyone else. Over all those years, thirty albums isn't really so much. You could make five albums a year, easily – ask any truly creative person. Even now. Most great ideas never even see the light of day. And each record is just what you did that week: another week you might have done the same songs differently. But listen – I loved every last one of them. Every single second of every last one, OK?"

Good to know. When I tell Lou that the legendary 1972 recording of himself, John Cale and Nico at The Bataclan, Paris was recently released, I'm stunned that he's stunned. "That's on the market? That's available in the UK? Well we need to get an injunction out quick against that. They have no right to put that out without the say-so of all the parties involved."

Seeking less incendiary ground – there must be some *somewhere* – I encourage him to talk about *Animal Serenade* for a while. Is it in any way a companion piece to his famously heavy live album *Rock'n'Roll Animal*, a record that defined "rock" before the Darkness were in nappies?

"Hey well, it's the thirtieth anniversary of *Rock'n'Roll Animal*," he announces cheerily. "And this one's a serenade, yes, but an *animal* serenade. At least that's my thinking. It's technically excellent." He's on about the sound quality. "If you're making records, it seems crazy not to want them to sound good. I realise everybody's going over to lo-fi now. But that's an understandable reaction against slick pop. But what about having

lo-fi that's hi-fi? You get me? Lo-fi that's recorded exquisitely. Any musician spends their whole life trying to get a great sound – otherwise, why bother? You'd get pleasure out of looking at a beautiful painting, so why wouldn't you want the same with sound? Unless you're deaf. In which case it's not your fault."

Asked how he chose which songs to play here, Lou says he handed the decision to the other musicians. "Everybody put down their favourites. I may have had some input. Maybe. It just seemed a good opportunity to readdress some songs, use the cello, and not have them drowned out by drums. To bring them closer. And you can hear the words. I've been to a lotta shows where the artist seems to assume the audience knows all the words, so they're not clear. I don't consider that right. You should be able to hear the words." There's no "Perfect Day" here, no "Walk On The Wild Side", probably because Lou's milked them countless times over other live albums.

"Y'know what, though? They just approached me about doing a remix of *Transformer*. That oughtta be fun. We could put Bowie's saxophone right at the back. We could mess around a whole lot."

Reed's also re-recorded *Metal Machine Music*, live, in the Berlin Philharmonic Hall. "It's awesome. We may just release it in the States." For the uninitiated, *Metal Machine Music* was the ultimate anti-music noise, the

John The Baptist of Punk. An unlistenable litany of howls and screeches. Or, obviously, a pioneering, fearless work of genius. "Turns out it's not so far-out for audiences now. It's not nearly so: oh my God, what's that?! They can stay with it. It just goes 100mph all the way."

And then stops?

"In a way, it never really stops."

"The Day John Kennedy Died" is revisited on *Animal Serenade*. "I thought it was appropriate when somebody like George Bush was in … uh … 'power'."

Could John Kerry be the new JFK?

"Oh, how would I know?"

Well, you're closer to it in America than …

"Nobody's closer to it. They keep us all well away. It's smoke and mirrors, all of them. But just – anybody but Bush, is the thing. Anybody but Bush."

Asked if he still abides by Andy Warhol's work ethic, Reed sighs almost vulnerably. "I'm not even close. Much as I try, much as I'm busy, I could never match that." The single greatest influence on his writing, he reaffirms, was Delmore Schwartz, the late poet-novelist who was his professor at college. "Spiritually

and lyrically, it was Delmore's short story 'In Dreams Begin Responsibilities'. That made me go, wow, without a crazy vocabulary you can hit the widest range imaginable. Or you can go where Hubert Selby goes, or Raymond Chandler. Then naturally you try and go your own way. Or at least I hope I did. And do. I saw these giants, and …"

Aimed high?

"Mmm. And low. High and low both."

His new photography book *Emotion In Action* gives each photo no title. "Given the extent to which writing words is part of what I do, it'd be intrusive. Leading the witness. See them for yourself, ask your own questions." And the meditation music? "I made it to do t'ai chi to, and friends asked for it. Y'know, no major label is gonna put this out, so I just made up a few copies. If people go to my website, if they're interested, they can follow it up. That's the joy of the Internet. If they ask for it, I'm not gonna say no."

As ever, talking to Lou Reed has been a tense, nervous and stressful joy. Is it true you once said you were too smart and literate to be "the godfather of punk"?

"I said that? No. No way. C'mon, you can't believe that shit, you know that shit ain't true. Why would I say that? That's crazy. Look at what I write. C'mon, I mean – I've been in jail, y'know?"

INTRODUCTION

➤ WALK ON THE WILD SIDE ➤

"I've hidden behind the MYTH of Lou Reed for years. I can blame anything outrageous on HIM. I make believe sometimes that I'm Lou Reed. I'm so easily seduced by the public image of Lou Reed that I'm in love with Lou Reed myself. I think he's wonderful. No, it's not something I do to disguise my vulnerability or insecurity. Sometimes I just like being Lou Reed better than I like being anyone else."

Lou Reed, 1977 *Melody Maker* interview with Allan Jones.

On his latest live album, *Animal Serenade*, 62-year-old Lou Reed, as is his wont, talks between songs, in that inimitable cynical drawl of his. At one stage, introducing the emaciated but epic "Street Hassle", he makes grand, borderline pompous, claims for his talents: "I wanted to write a song that mixed up William Burroughs, Nelson Algren, Tennessee Williams, Hubert Selby Jr, maybe a little Raymond Chandler. You mix 'em all up, you have 'Street Hassle'." But earlier in the album, he's acknowledged that his legacy may be less highbrow. It may be that he's remembered and

revered as "the Godfather of Punk", a man who made much mileage of a few facile chords. "So, I thought I'd explain to you how to make a career out of three chords," he snarls as this set begins. "You younger bands, pay attention. You thought it was three? Ha! It's really four!" He teases out the seminal riff of "Sweet Jane", proving it's the fourth that makes it sting. "As with most things in life," he smirks, "it's that little hop at the end …"

Reed has always been a chaos of contradictions. Of course we love the fact that this narcissistic genius/fool worships the twin poles of high poetry and simple three-chord (sorry, four-chord) trash. That's the way it should be. "I love Lou," the late Sterling Morrison once commented, "but he has what must be a fragmented personality. You're never too sure, under any conditions, what you're going to have to deal with."

"I'd harboured the hope that the intelligence that once inhabited novels and films would ingest rock," Reed himself once said. "I was, perhaps, wrong."

We'll see about that.

Impossible as it is to summarise his sometimes brilliant, sometimes baffling solo career without

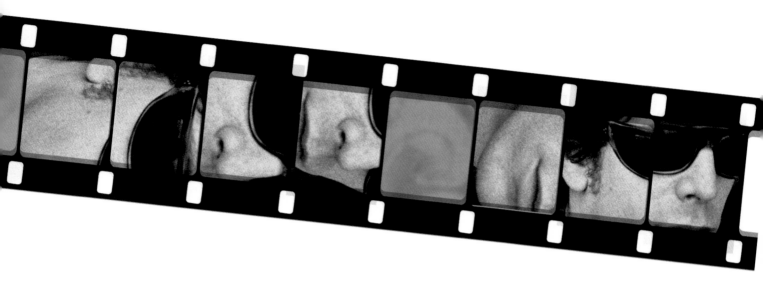

careering into a pyramid of paradoxes, even the most cursory scan of his durable recorded output reveals a determined, almost perverse passion for wearing his brain on his sleeve. He's been fiercely intellectual when it was out of vogue, and crazily dumb when he was out of his head. His image, many times remoulded, once thrived on a potent, dangerous edginess – a sassy, sussed streetwise punk playing with gender roles – yet now seems settled as bespectacled neo-librarian, a self-important academic hunkering down with hubris, a revisionist who denies most of his actions throughout the '70s. He's been art-rocker, iconoclast, gutter poet, white-noise merchant and junkie prophet. The Phantom of Rock, the Godfather of Punk. ("I'm too literate to be into punk rock," he snapped in 1977. "My current designation is ridiculous. I don't think I'm responsible for anything.") Few people, if any, will love his entire body of work: his oeuvre has often been challenging and on occasion downright unlistenable (*Metal Machine Music*, anyone?), while at other times he's proven himself a master of

melody and the songwriter's craft. "My bullshit is other people's diamonds," he's famously said. And, "My week beats your year." He's alienated supporters with his abrasive attitude, yet penned subversive sing-along anthems like "Perfect Day" and the recently revamped "Satellite of Love". He's courted controversial subjects, from sniggering sex, decadent drugs and visceral violence, to po-faced prayers to Poe and that final countdown, death. His was a turbulent youth; as a sexagenarian he's still a less than cosy figure.

If he's rarely taken the world by storm commercially, it's difficult to deny his standing as a colossus of the rock world. His influence has coloured decades of the darker music (insert list of your favourite bands here). He's the daddy of outsiders, losers, misfits. In a field where the word legend is bandied around like it's going out of style, his own remains imperishable. He's an icon of cool, a sinning saint of rebellion.

He's won over admirers and collaborators with his gifts; isolated them with his notorious temper. To many, he *is* New York. "I operate on instinct a lot," he's said. "I don't question it. I'm just glad I have it."

The Velvet Underground will always reign undisputed as one of the all-time great rock'n'roll bands, with many convinced their radical invention and reckless courage probed the heart of unease that the Beatles or the Stones shied away from. Perhaps the received wisdom of the rock canon will forever declare that Reed's subsequent solo work has never surpassed or even matched that unique '60s outfit's idiosyncratic explosion/implosion of sound and imagery. The sinister, glamorously decadent aura of the Velvets has been hugely inflated – a grubby, off-silver balloon – by that of Andy Warhol and the attendant Factory scene of the era.

Yet to some of us, Reed's erratic solo work, particularly early on, has included even more magical moments since that immortal band's initial demise. Maybe it's time to attempt to analyse, celebrate, pump up and shoot down the rabid intelligence and literary merits of Lou Reed's post-Velvets music, its flourishes and its follies. The purple Bowie-blessed pop of *Transformer*. The tortuous tragic grandeur of *Berlin*, the no-holds-barred storytelling of *Street Hassle* or the record that once again revived his ailing reputation, *New York*. The cheeky, caustic confessionals of *Coney Island Baby* and *Growing Up In Public*. Those curiously popular live albums. The simultaneous languor and unrest of *The Blue Mask*, a study of love and fear; the intimations of mortality which informed the near-heroic but improbably dreary *Magic And Loss*. And the turkeys – there have been plenty. This account will be largely subjective: we will get highly excited about the '70s albums, then appear to bash through the later releases as if they're not all that important. That's the response they inspire in us, honestly. We focus on his most vibrant, purple period, where his music does stuff, when raging attitude was more important than refined craftsmanship.

Ferocious, lazy, prickly, melancholy, overtly heterosexual, flamboyantly camp, Reed's been nothing if not erratic, but when he was in the zone – a private purgatory, probably – he caught fire and found a way to channel it. His long walk on the wild side has been some journey, and every step, from wise-ass one-liner to nonchalant non sequitur, from all-time great album to awfully timed grating album, from decade to decade, tells us something about the state of the art of rock'n'roll.

"I guess that I'm dumb 'cos I know I'm not smart," he drawled in 1976. "But deep down inside I've got a rock'n'roll heart." In 2000, he sang, "I'm the only one left standing."

Licentious libertine looking for a good time or bookish boffin bewildering his awed acolytes, Reed has been one of the genre's prime poets and pugilists, both victim and visionary. His has been a hell of a life, as crammed with conflict and crescendo as his music. Let's take that walk.

Sterling Morrison, Mo Tucker, Lou Reed, John Cale

© GERARD MALANGA, 1966

BEGINNING TO SEE THE LIGHT:

Lou Reed and the
Velvet Underground

(1972)

Lewis Allan Reed was born in Brooklyn, New York, on 2 March 1942. Or possibly Louis Firbank was born on the same date in 1943, or even 1944, in Freeport, Long Island. It depends who you believe. You're going to have to get used to this, and you may as well get used to it early on. In the '70s, as he finally gained some commercial success, his record company openly admitted to journalists that they were afraid to pin him down on the question. His wordless glare can be deeply intimidating. Mo Tucker, the Velvets' drummer, swore by the first version, as do the majority of commentators, so we'll go with Mo.

It's generally agreed that there was a younger sister, Elizabeth, and a brother born a decade later. Reed's father, Sidney, ran a legal accountancy firm; his mother, Toby, is said to have been a former beauty queen. Dad's business thrived, and when Reed was eleven it seems the family moved upmarket from Brooklyn to Freeport, near Coney Island. Cue *Coney Island Baby* references. Beaches, boardwalks, funfairs. Asked years later if he was Jewish (because he'd been insulting the Jewish race, specifically his Jewish manager), Reed answered, "Of course: aren't all the best people?" He's claimed his parents were self-made millionaires, and added, "I didn't want to grow up like my old man." To this point, Reed can't "blame" anything on a tough childhood. He tried to be sporty. He wasn't too hot. Being middle class, he was given classical piano lessons. He studied theory, composition, the avant-garde. For the rest of his life, depending on what kind of record he was releasing, he would either dismiss this technical grounding as "boring, I forgot it all", or flag it up proudly to prove his credentials. He was already writing poems too, and composing, with his cousin, pastiches of rockabilly and doo-wop.

Then came the troublesome teenage years. Instantly sussing that you could play nearly everything you heard on the radio with three chords,

Reed joined a succession of bands at school. He first recorded with the Shades, later the Jades. A single – "Leave Her For Me"/ "So Blue" – was released on Dot Records. The writer's credit? Lewis Reed. The single did nothing. The band played shopping malls.

The adolescent Reed wasn't enjoying the experience as much as he'd have liked. He realised he was sexually attracted to his own gender, and covering it up was extremely stressful, "a very big drag". His parents, becoming aware of this, were mortified. It was the late '50s; Senator McCarthy was instilling fear and loathing of "subversives" and "hoodlums". In a working-class family, the seventeen-year-old Reed would probably have had his homosexual tendencies beaten and kicked out of him. Such were the times. However his well-off, conservative parents took a decision that has brought them much criticism, not least from their boy in his lyrics, ever since. They sent him for electroshock therapy, three times a week. That's what was recommended then. The effect, Reed said, was that "you lose your memory and become a vegetable". He wrote the song "Kill Your Sons" about it (but couldn't record it till about a decade later). Amateur psychologists can have a field day here: Reed from then on (until much later in life) railed against his parents and suburbia, was prone to anger and mood swings, latched on to a series of substitute father figures (only to rebel each time), and wrote arresting lyrics about pain, distress and murky sexuality.

He threw himself further into music. By the fall of 1961, the nineteen-year-old Reed escaped to Syracuse University, two hundred miles northwest. He took a BA degree in literature and philosophy. Hegel, Kierkegaard and French Existentialism were big: the freedom and fear of meaninglessness simultaneously appalled and appealed to the intellectual within the rhythm guitarist. Like most students, he also closely studied sex, drugs and rock'n'roll.

One of his lecturers was the legendary if declining

author and poet Delmore Schwartz. After early acclaim for his groundbreaking 1937 book *In Dreams Begin Responsibilities*, Schwartz had become an increasingly frustrated, paranoid, self-obsessed figure. A sparkling conversationalist, described by Reed as "incredibly smart", he was addicted to drink and speed by the time he landed – thanks to the loyal backing of Saul Bellow and Robert Lowell – a lectureship post at Syracuse in 1962. There, within 48 hours, he was arrested for drunkenness. Still quite the raconteur, he'd regale his students in the bar with anecdotes about the sex lives of James Joyce, T.S. Eliot and – insanely – Queen Elizabeth II. He took a shine to the awestruck Reed, giving him signed copies of his books and introducing him to Dostoevsky. He encouraged Reed's poetry, and scared him with stories of what he'd do if Reed ever "sold out". He was one of the most influential characters in Reed's early life, even making a cameo as a ghost on 1982's *The Blue Mask*.

The aspiring poet had his work rejected by

magazines, but consoled himself by presenting a jazz show on college radio (imagine that voice giving you the time checks). He called his show *Excursion On A Wobbly Rail*, after an improvisational piece by Cecil Taylor. As well as doo-wop and Sun Records rock'n'roll, he'd play plenty of Ornette Coleman and Don Cherry (both of whom he'd record with years later). He got seriously into drugs, contracting hepatitis from a shared needle. He'd later quip, "The Beatles were innocent of the world and its wicked ways, while I no longer possessed this pristine view. I, after all, had jaundice." The seeds of a song called "Heroin" were sown.

Reed signed up to take a postgraduate course, first studying journalism but then switching to drama. He packed in the journalism studies after they criticised him for "interjecting an opinion". As a drama student, he played the part of a dead body. Around this time, he met a guitarist friend of a friend, going on to play in several student bands with him. His name was Sterling Morrison. The friend of a friend was Jim Tucker, who had a sister named Maureen, who liked to play the drums.

One of these not-overly-earnest student groups, in various permutations, played bars and fraternities, Reed later claiming he made more money at such unglamorous venues than he ever did with the Velvet Underground. He dodged the Vietnam draft. He's since given various different reasons. Hepatitis. Homosexuality. Mental unfitness. He's said that everyone he knew was evading the war in any way possible, but later admitted to recognising a moral dilemma there. Instead of fighting, by late 1964 and early 1965 he'd gone to work at Pickwick Records' office in New York.

Here, his job was to churn out jingles, ditties and rip-offs of current hits to be flogged on supermarket-targeted albums under fictitious band names: the Roughnecks, the Beachnuts, the All Night Workers. He continued working on his own writing in his own time. A potentially awkward

Clockwise from top left: Mo Tucker, Lou Reed, Sterling Morrison and John Cale

scenario occurred when one of the label's nonexistent bands – the Primitives – "enjoyed" minor success, and were asked to appear on the popular television show *American Bandstand*. Their song was a demented parody of the current boom in dance crazes, called "The Ostrich". To dance the ostrich, you apparently had to "put your head on the floor and have somebody step on it". Reed and colleague Terry Phillips couldn't turn down this opportunity, and cobbled together a "band" with two guys Terry met at a party. They were Tony Conrad and his flatmate, who was the classically trained son of a Welsh miner, a child prodigy who was in New York on a scholarship to Tanglewood, a renowned music college. His interest in the avant-garde captivated Reed: his name was John Cale.

The Primitives didn't last long, but Reed and Cale continued to collaborate, along with Sterling Morrison and percussionist Angus MacLise. Through 1965, they played under short-lived names such as the Warlocks and the Falling Spikes. An underground filmmaker, Piero Heliczer, asked them to contribute music for a short movie he'd made, named *Venus In Furs*. Reed looked at the "kinky" book of the same name by Leopold Von Sacher-Masoch, and, simply loving the title, thought this a splendid idea. "Now," he sighed later, "everyone thinks I invented masochism." The drummer disappeared to India, so Maureen Tucker was brought in ("We needed an amplifier, and she had one."). The Velvet Underground played their first ever show on 12 December 1965, at Summit High School, New Jersey. They supported a band called Myddle (sic) Class. Tony Conrad showed Reed and Cale another "subversive" book – Michael Leigh's meretricious sex exposé, *The Velvet Underground*. The four members of the band all agreed this would make a fine name. They played a few nights at the Café Bizarre in Greenwich Village, their set a mixture of Reed's darkly worded songs (given avant-garde twists by Cale) and Chuck

Berry covers. They were soon sacked by the venue, but not before Andy Warhol had seen them there.

Warhol was already a phenomenon, a widely celebrated pop artist. His boldly cold, pioneering work in painting, performance art and experimental films lacked, he felt, a rock band to reflect his images and ideas sonically. When he offered the Velvet Underground a management contract within days of their first meeting, they – although too full of their own original ideas to be anybody's puppets – decided this was a merger worth gambling on. He was famous (or notorious) and extremely hip; they weren't. He offered money, equipment, and rehearsal space. He'd want them to play any "events" he organised upon demand. They signed the deal before the year was out. In 1966, they began to make history.

Although this book is to focus chiefly on Lou Reed's solo career, the taboos and themes tangled with by the Velvet Underground – not to mention the mythology still surrounding the band – reoccur throughout his later writing, and served to make him a shadowy lord of cool, counter-culture charisma, before that solo career even began. It's one of rock music's best-loved axioms that not many people bought a Velvet Underground record, but everyone that heard one went out and formed a band.

"Andy told me that what we were doing with music," Reed has said, "was the same thing he was doing with painting, movies and writing – i.e. not kidding around. We were doing a specific thing that was very, very real. It wasn't slick or a lie in any conceivable way. All the songs were written before I met him – it's just that they happened to match his thing perfectly."

Reed began to hang around Warhol's infamous New York studio, the Factory, digging the scene and the flamboyant "Warhol superstars", borrowing aspects of their attitude and dress sense, admiring Andy's work ethic. Many of these eccentric characters were to turn up in later songs, not least

"Walk On The Wild Side". It's even been said that Reed took to being monosyllabic and only minimally communicative in conversation because he so admired that trait in Warhol. Yet Warhol deemed that something was still missing from the Velvet Underground, and that something was "The Pop Girl of '66", as he promoted her – Nico.

Former model and actress (she appeared in Fellini's *La Dolce Vita*) Nico had been born in Hungary to Spanish/Yugoslav parents, and spoke seven languages. But she turned down a potentially lucrative contract with Fellini when she met Bob Dylan, who introduced her to Warhol. Warhol thought the Velvets boys needed an extra dose of onstage charisma. The Velvets boys didn't, so trouble was already brewing. It didn't help that there was no love lost between the rival Warhol and Dylan camps, and that Nico kept demanding to sing a song Dylan had written for her, "I'll Keep It With Mine". Reed dismissed Dylan's lyrics as "marijuana throwaways, that didn't mean anything". He was now drawing welcome attention for his own lyrics and their gritty, candid, confrontational imagery of losers self-destructing through various addictions and excesses. He was hailed for the first time as a street poet, shattering cosy middle-class preconceptions. But if someone was dumb enough to take heroin just because they heard a song, he barked ominously, it wasn't his responsibility.

With Andy full of colourful plans, the band tolerated Nico's presence. The Velvet Underground And Nico debuted at the Delmonico Hotel in New York on 8 January. However it was their appearance at Warhol's mixed-media event "Up-Tight", in February, which really got the city's underground buzzing. This led to arguably his and their finest live moment – The Exploding Plastic Inevitable. A potent mix of theatrical extravaganza and perverse performance art, it's become the stuff of legend. Strobes and spotlights dazzled, films flickered, car horns honked, dancers writhed as if

their lives depended on it, and the distinctive rock'n'roll feedback of the Velvets pierced hysterically through it all. Criticised by some as "grotesque", Reed quietly asserted it was "fun". "Revolutionary", opined Warhol. "Camp plus con", snarled one newspaper. Reed and Cale wore wraparound sunglasses to shield their eyes from the lights. And something practical came out of this: when the show was banned in LA, the band were paid anyway. They spent the money on a recording session there. Tom Wilson produced, though Warhol was credited as producer as a marketing device. Among the tracks recorded: "Waiting For The Man", "All Tomorrow's Parties", "Venus In Furs", "Heroin" and "Sunday Morning". The subsequent album – *The Velvet Underground And Nico* – bore a phallic banana design (by Warhol) on the sleeve, and was to become one of the landmark albums of rock'n'roll. Not yet though – the MGM Verve label sat on it until spring of the next year, choosing to prioritise Frank Zappa. Which explains why Reed has taken snidey potshots at Zappa ever since. When the record finally did emerge – "you've got to keep the dirty words in," asserted Warhol – it didn't sell, reaching No. 171 in the US charts. Outside their immediate switched-on, clued-up circle, the band weren't going to be quickly

appreciated or understood. Still, they were making ripples. And, of course, the album's influence on generations of musicians since is incalculable.

Relationships within the group were growing more fractious. Reed and Cale, neither of them short on ego, each considered themselves the star, the focal point. At the time they failed to realise how greatly their visions complemented and inspired each other. Tours – always drug-fuelled – were gruelling. In mid-1967 they played Boston and, with Warhol at the Cannes Film Festival and Nico away nurturing a solo career, decided it was time for major changes. When a proposed deal with Beatles manager Brian Epstein fell through, they signed with young club owner Steve Sesnick. Warhol was distraught, felt betrayed, and called Reed "a rat". Nico actually tried to clamber onstage with the group at one gig, but, humiliatingly, they wouldn't let her. Their second album, *White Light/White Heat*, recorded again with Tom Wilson in California, came out at the tail end of 1967. It soared to No. 199 on the *Billboard* chart. Screechy, aggressive, it was dominated by the seventeen-minute one-take wonder that was "Sister Ray", and the verbose, enigmatic "The Gift". Although things were relatively patched up with Warhol by now, enough for him to provide the original artwork for the album, Sesnick was egging Reed on to go solo. Cale was highly irritated, and personalities were clashing left, right and centre. Something had to give. It turned out to be John Cale.

Ideals of democracy were forgotten as Reed and Sesnick began to dictate what and where the band should play. The music became more commercial (relatively!) and conservative, allowing the prettier, more melodic side of Reed's songwriting to reign. Morrison has said that Reed wanted more emphasis on his lyrics, while he and Cale were still keen on "blasting the house down". Cale married fashion designer Betsey Johnson, and this

Nico: the band "tolerated" her presence

Warhol was shot by Factory fringe freak Valerie Solanis – his health was always fragile from then on, and his art lurched towards safer havens. Reed was shocked, but by August 1968 had recovered his ruthlessness sufficiently to call a band meeting (without Cale) where he demanded Cale's exit from the Velvets. Morrison and Tucker, by their own admission, put self-interest first and sold John out. Cale has since held the stance that the band wasn't big enough for the both of them, although in his sacking's immediate aftermath, he more bitterly proclaimed: "It was just a flash in the pan. It came and it went … we never really fulfilled our potential. With tracks like 'Heroin', 'Venus In Furs', 'All Tomorrow's Parties' and 'Sister Ray' we defined a completely new way of working. It was without precedent. Drugs, and the fact that no one gave a damn about us, meant we gave up on it too soon."

Cale went on to an impressive career of making much-admired, left-field music, and producing significant artists from the Stooges and Nico to Patti Smith to Happy Mondays. The Velvet Underground were – whether Reed yet recognised it or not – in irreversible decline. "I only hope John will go on to be recognised as the Beethoven of his day," said Reed, in a rare moment of magnanimity.

The band's third album was self-produced, and plainly titled *The Velvet Underground*. It came out in March 1969, with the young and impressionable (and therefore highly malleable) Doug Yule brought in to replace the unique Cale as well as a promising, jobbing musician could. Reed encouraged Yule to sing Reed's lyrics – "I'm sure he never understood a word" – while Morrison bemoaned the fact that many of the songs seemed to be veering towards the sentimental and referencing their author's old girlfriend in Syracuse. "If I wrote a song like that," he said, "I wouldn't make you play it." Still, the gently psychedelic album contains several durable jewels, from "Candy Says" (which Reed still performs) to "What Goes On", from "Pale Blue Eyes" to "Beginning To See The Light". Reed saw it as a themed concept album, the stories of the songs interrelating, "a synopsis of sin", though for most listeners the literary thread is tricky to unravel. The record company were underwhelmed. The band, touring heavily, covertly touted for a new deal, recording plenty of material that – as events transpired – didn't see the light for years afterwards. These "lost" works popped up as *VU* in 1985 and *Another VU* in 1986. Their next release, *Loaded*, in September 1970, was pretty much a death rattle, albeit one which contained such classics as "Sweet Jane", "Rock And Roll" and "Who Loves The Sun". It was marginally more radio-friendly, but the Velvet Underground were never destined to cut it as a dirtier version of the Monkees. Mo Tucker, pregnant, had now been replaced by Doug Yule's brother Billy, and Doug was singing more than Lou

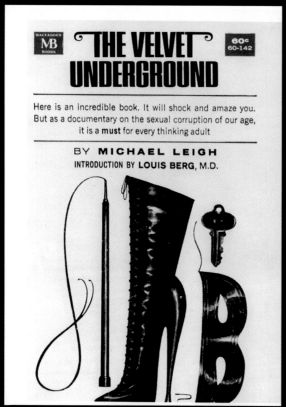

COURTSEY OF GERARD MALANGA COLLECTION, 1963

(ostensibly because Lou was screwing up his voice with excessive live commitments). Reed disowned *Loaded*, claiming the editing had chopped the best songs (especially "Sweet Jane" and "New Age") to ribbons. "Sheer stupidity, blatant stupidity … I just gave up on it, I wasn't there when it was done."

Reed and Sesnick were now at loggerheads, and after a flurry of shows at Max's Kansas City (the last of which, in August 1970, was fortuitously recorded by Warhol acolyte Brigid Polk and eventually released in 1972 as *Live At Max's Kansas City*), Reed walked. Reportedly now a speed freak existing on six hours' sleep a week, and increasingly paranoid, depressed and defensive, he still had foggy notions of a solo career. Constant exhaustion and bouts of hepatitis didn't bode well. Though the Velvets nominally puttered on with Doug Yule at the helm (until as late as 1973, when the *Squeeze* album was universally panned), the legend as we perceive it was over – at least, until over twenty years later. "It was a process of elimination from the start," an older, arguably wiser, Reed mused. "First no more Andy, then no more Nico, then no more John, then no more Velvet Underground."

"If it wasn't me," he later confessed, "I would have idolised myself in the Velvets. I loved what we did and I'm proud of it. We stood for everything that kids loved and adults hated. We were loud, you couldn't understand the lyrics, we were vulgar, we sang about dope, sex, violence – you name it. But it wasn't the 'nocturnal side' of rock'n'roll – it was the daylight side. No one else had noticed it, that's all. It didn't take nerve to write those songs… we couldn't understand the reaction, we didn't know why everyone was reeling in shock. If you line the songs up chronologically, you should be able to relate and not feel alone. I think it's important that people don't feel alone."

Lewis Allan Reed, pushing thirty, jaded and jaundiced, was about to spend some time alone. Well, he would've been, if he hadn't gone back to live with his parents in Long Island, taking a job with his father's accountancy company. There, while pondering his next move and using his father's know-how to extricate himself from various legal and contractual complications, he typed. He sneakily won the rights to most of the Velvets' material, a coup which Morrison and Cale found less than thrilling. He wrote poetry, and met Bettye, a waitress/wannabe actress. Privately, he told friends he'd never sing in public again. He'd retired. It wasn't as if a nation mourned (in the UK he was still practically unknown). Those few who cared revved the rock'n'roll rumour mill into overdrive – where was the great be-shaded enigma? And what was he on? The mundane truth is that for two years, he was a typist. For his dad.

And there – before it really began – the story could've ended, were it not for the intervention of, among other true believers, one David Bowie.

© GERARD MALANGA, 1975

THE LOU REED ALBUMS

LOU REED
July (1972)

I CAN'T STAND IT ❯ GOING DOWN ❯ **WALK AND TALK IT** ❯ LISA SAYS ❯ **BERLIN** ❯ I LOVE YOU ❯ **WILD CHILD** ❯ LOVE MAKES YOU FEEL ❯ **RIDE INTO THE SUN** ❯ OCEAN ❯ **Produced:** Richard Robinson and Lou Reed **Recorded at:** Morgan Studios, London **Musicians:** Lou Reed (vocals, guitar); Caleb Quaye (guitars, piano); Steve Howe (electric guitar); Paul Keogh (guitars); Rick Wakeman (piano); Les Hurdle (bass); Brian Odgers (bass); Clem Cattini (percussion); Kay Garner (vocals); Helene Francois (vocals).

The review in *Rolling Stone* of Lou Reed's first solo album was, unlike most other reviews, kind. Gushing, even. "Almost perfect," it hollered. "First-rate rock and roll music." While the consensus now – correctly – is that *Lou Reed* was a necessary interim step, a dry run or forgiven false start on the swift learning curve between the Velvet Underground and the commercial carnal candy of the subsequent *Transformer*, it is far from perfect, poorly produced, and second rate. Reed reworks a bunch of songs mostly written for the Velvets, but with a bunch of showy session musicians who don't connect with his psyche at all.

And yet at times – on the few occasions when the album does click, when it flies, as in the exhilarating climax of "Love Makes You Feel" or the proto-punk stomp of "I Can't Stand It" – it's joyful and highly likeable. It's also an interesting insight into where Reed's head was at during this period, with its mix of sketchy wrath and sweet, innocent, "uncharacteristic" love songs, staunchly apolitical, flavoured by his covert fondness for soul and standard pop.

"One chord is fine. Two chords are pushing it," Reed has said, attempting to define rock'n'roll. "Three chords and you're into jazz."

Tellingly, if controversially, that *Rolling Stone* review, after a handy pocket history (a kind of "Previously, on The Lou Reed Story ..."), is keen to vote Reed over Cale. "Was it really as far back as 1965 that the Velvets were discovered by Andy Warhol and toured the country with his mixed-media freakshow, The Exploding Plastic Inevitable? Back then their music was overshadowed by their pervy image and the spectre of Camp that engulfed Warhol at the time. Only later did many people realise that the Velvets were not just making the loudest noise ever before heard, they were making some of the best rock and roll in America. It's all there on their first album, the one with the peelable banana on the cover. And today it sounds fresher than ever – like the early Stones." Continues critic Stephen Holden, "For my money, it is *the* classic New York rock album of the Sixties. On subsequent albums the Velvets never got it quite so together again, though each one contained at least a couple of memorable tracks – enough for them to acquire a loyal cult following. Now Reed's first solo effort shows that he, more than John Cale (master of the sound of disintegration), embodied the spirit of the Velvets. It... contains some of the grittiest rock sounds being laid down today. It is skeletal rock – sexy, pimply, crude and sophisticated, all at the same time. Reed's voice hasn't changed much since the early days. Outrageously unmusical, it combines the sass of Jagger and the mockery of early Dylan but is lower-pitched than either. It is a voice so incapable of bullshit that it makes even an artsy arrangement work by turning the whole thing into a joyous travesty."

Well put, although in the next passage the musicians are described as sounding "like they've played together for years". Yeah, Scrabble maybe, or bridge. The multiple guitarists indulge in a horrendously dated dick-swinging contest from start

David Bowie: "glam" was emerging

to finish which all but blots Reed out. It's some kind of testament to his, uh, distinctive voice (and witty lyrics) that at least a small fraction of his personality survives to be heard. With his fiendish subversion of the yearnings of classic '50s teen laments, and his ability to make the fevered freaks of his tales come to life before our very ears, Reed here tugs and tramples out a personal clearing in the long grass of the '70s' swiftly evolving times. In the words of "Ocean", here come the waves.

The music business in the early '70s was in transition. The original rock audience was growing up, while the next generation wanted their own icons, not those of their parents or elder siblings. Many artists had to feel their way for a while, work out what was required of them if they were to stay in the game. Rock and pop were polarised between age groups. The Beatles had split, Dylan was semi-retired, Jimi Hendrix, Jim Morrison and Janis Joplin had all turned out to be poor adverts for drug abuse. Gentler, California-based soft rock (Neil Young, Joni Mitchell, James Taylor) dominated America, while in the UK the inexplicable popularity of pretentious fourteen-hour triple concept albums by indulgent prog-rock outfits was about to be blown away by the sheer energy and pizazz of Marc Bolan, David Bowie and glam, or Glitter rock. The taboos toppled by all things Warhol were just beginning to filter through to the quaint little European island.

Meanwhile, in his temporary isolation, Lou Reed was learning that he wasn't an island. First, he fell in love. Probably, this inspired some songs. Certainly, it inspired some dodgy poetry. Bettye – a neat blonde in twinset and pearls who Reed's parents adored – was an unlikely partner for the decadent bisexual Factory burnout who wrote of degradation and horror. Yet it seems her conventionality was just what he sought … for now. His poetry of the period is more confessional and intimate – about his own feelings, rather than those of others observed with detachment – than that of any other time in his life.

But he wasn't ready for the white picket fence just yet. In the early summer of 1971, he found himself seduced by the rock world again. Drinking with eager fans Richard and Lisa Robinson – a record producer/former critic and his wife, also a rock journalist – he was encouraged to get back in the ring and record his songs. He took some persuading, but the pair were persistent. Though his repertoire was largely Velvets leftovers, he was proud and protective. Sessions in London were organised, where a groundswell of interest in Reed was forming. Rising star David Bowie had been performing Velvets songs live, and lauding Warhol on his *Hunky Dory* album – much more was to come of this mutual appreciation, as was to become abundantly evident with Reed's second album, *Transformer*. Ironically, Reed knew that his links with Warhol were proving to be a commercial kiss of death Stateside. He was smart to capitalise on his British hipness.

Richard Robinson pressed the case for recording in London, and Reed chose Morgan Studios in Willesden because Rod Stewart had made the *Every Picture Tells A Story* album there. Alarmingly conventional compared to the Velvets' brightest-burning moments, Reed now declared that his favourite acts were Rod, the Stones and Chuck Berry. Given that, it's less bizarre than it might seem that the session men recruited by Robinson included Steve Howe and Rick Wakeman from the then about-to-happen pompous noodlers Yes (Wakeman had recently played with Bowie on the *Space Oddity* and *Hunky Dory* albums). Guitarist Caleb Quaye was an erstwhile Elton John sidekick who played with the British band Hookfoot, and drummer Clem Cattini was a living legend who can be heard on both "Shakin' All Over" by Johnny Kidd and the Pirates and "Telstar" by the Tornados. Robinson roped in two – in his words – "chick singers", to give the sound a "soul" feel. Given that Robinson had previously produced two potent enough records for San Francisco band the

Flamin' Groovies, and wasn't a novice, it's astonishing how vapid the production ended up being on *Lou Reed*. Reed, whose guitar style didn't gel with these consummate musos, didn't play on it.

Bankrolled by a generous RCA, Reed – still overindulging in drink and drugs and therefore pudgily overweight, as photographs from the era demonstrate – was booked into some of London's most expensive hotels and more than adequately looked after. He played the mystique-laden rock-

Rick Wakeman, caped crusader

legend role because, here, it was not only encouraged but believed in. Besotted with both Bettye and (it's said) Richard Robinson, who he introduced as "my girlfriend… and my boyfriend", he distractedly assumed a bunch of old, orphaned songs would suffice for the album. The musicians shrugged and did what they could, with Robinson too overawed to give them direction. Reed wanted both to show he could record without being "difficult", and to get back to the hotel suite and get wrecked, and so he just got on with it, uncomplainingly. Lou, Bettye and the Robinsons hung out together round the clock, forming their own self-bolstering clique. When Reed later clinically dumped the Robinsons for new management, they were mortified. Reed was already establishing a pattern for using people then dropping them. Only with hindsight is it clear that he tends to drop too soon (Cale, Bowie). Listening to Robinson's tinpot production, however, you have to concede that in this case he had a very valid point.

"I don't have a personality of my own," he declared at the time. "I just pick up on other people's." Between the Warhol era and the too-brief Bowie era, we can only assume this album was coloured by the personalities of Bettye and Mr & Mrs Robinson. And while sessions were drawing to a close, Reed flew to Paris in January 1972 for an extraordinary turnaround. There he performed an acoustic set at the Bataclan Club, alongside – for the first time in three years – Nico and John Cale. They rang mournfully through some old Velvets favourites, Cale's electric viola infusing any energy. Lou actually made murmurs about reforming, but at this time both Cale and Nico's solo careers were doing promisingly enough without him, thank you very much. Still, the show served to fuel the Velvets myth, which continued to grow in Europe.

With the album finished, Reed returned to the States and put a touring band together for an American tour timed to coincide with the record's release. He chose to team up with a generic bar band, the Tots, described by Lester Bangs as "the ugliest cretins ever assembled on one stage … an intentionally asexual band". They played old songs, new songs, and Reed, introducing each number politely and formally, mustered a faint Mick Jagger impersonation, waving his arms around uncertainly. Album reviews were mixed, some as enthusiastic as the aforementioned *Rolling Stone* piece, others bemoaning the absence of Cale's ingenuity, of any sense of daring, of feedback and overt artiness. During promotional duties, a bloated, bleary-eyed Reed sometimes sent a roadie to give his interviews for him. Tragicomically, many didn't notice the difference.

"This is the closest realisation to what I hear in my head that I've ever done," Reed – assuming it wasn't an imposter – told *Disc and Music Echo*. "It's a real rock and roll album, and my direction has always been rock and roll – I see it as a life force. I don't think anybody who has been following my stuff is going to be surprised by what I've done here, plus I think the general audience will find it more accessible." Ever inconsistent, he was by October telling journalist/photographer Mick Rock: "There's just too many things wrong with it. I was in dandy form, and so was everyone else. I'm just aware of all the things that are missing, and all the things that shouldn't have been there."

The sleeve was a bombastic beauty, a specially commissioned painting by Tom Adams, whose covers for Raymond Chandler paperbacks had caught Reed's magpie eye. One other arresting aspect of Reed's promotional efforts, however, has survived, and deservedly. He self-penned a brief biog for RCA, and in doing so laid down the ground rules for the press presentation of his image. The press has willingly abided by it – and nurtured it – ever since. It read:

1. Played in Long Island hoodlum bands when there were fights.
2. Attended many schools – always had bands, i.e. Pasha and The Prophets, L.A. and The Eldorados.
3. Expelled from R.O.T.C. for threatening to shoot officer.
4. Rejected from army – deemed mentally unfit.
5. Worked as songwriter and met rejection.
6. Worked with Warhol and Velvet Underground through various permutations and helped create earlier "mixed media environment" also known in happy Sixties as "psychedelic".
7. Left Warhol, realigned band, and ultimately realigned self.
8. Exile and great pondering.
9. Lawsuits and depression.
10. RCA solo album. Satisfaction.

Hereby Reed set himself up as a fighter not an academic, a tough guy from the streets not a confused bisexual student of Dostoevsky. There had definitely been some realigning. Everyone who bought in to the myth bought it, but not many people bought the album. "Listening to it gives me the kind of charge I haven't had in God knows how long," wrote Richard Williams in *Melody Maker*. It "peaked" at No. 189 on the *Billboard* Top 200, selling around seven thousand copies – then considered paltry. There was yet much realigning to be done.

I CAN'T STAND IT

"We came for a change of pace," Reed told *Melody Maker* while in London. "We thought it'd be interesting to get out of the New York thing. We knew we'd be isolated – nobody comes into the studio, there's no great parties going on. It's just making a great rock'n'roll album." In truth, Reed, Robinson and their small but tight entourage were often holding court (on RCA's tab) at The Inn On The Park (then the expensive music biz hang-out of choice), and the reason the studio wasn't host to any great parties (on top of the fact that it was in unglamorous Willesden) was that Reed (usually intoxicated) and the English session men had little in common.

Ironically, the opening track, like "Wild Child", is New York through and through. A terrific burst of punky buzz-saw energy, with a timeless rock refrain about not being able to get any satisfaction, it's Chuck Berry through the Stones through (presciently) the Ramones. It's ripped, up for it, and it's a wonder it's rarely given due credit in the Reed canon. If the album had kept up this level of excitement, it's debatable whether *Transformer* would ever have needed to happen.

Lou sings like he's enjoying himself. He'd previously recorded the song (along with "Lisa Says", "Ocean" and "Ride Into The Sun") with the latterday Velvets – though those versions didn't see release until the '80s, and *VU* and *Another VU* (Reed, Morrison and Yule had roughly demoed others). His voice slopes confidently up for the chorus, encouraged by the oft-criticised but really rather fun backing vocals of Kay Garner and Helene Francois, and the drumming is like Mo Tucker on amphetamines. Reed's corny yelps of "It'll be all right now" and "Aw, c'mon baby!" are pure rock'n'roll cheesecake and are absolutely effective. The lead guitars (uncommonly, for this album) wait for the fade before overloading.

Having kicked in by proclaiming, "It's hard being a man, living in a garbage pail," Reed exits with a verse that's pretty much a concise summation of what rock'n'roll is all about: "I'm tired of living all alone/Nobody ever calls me on the phone/But when things start getting bad/I just play my music louder." There can be only one payoff after that: "I can't stand it any more more …"

Some curtain-raiser!

GOING DOWN

Half-heartedly leaked out as a US single, "Going Down" is a deceptively warm and gentle mid-tempo number, with Reed's voice remarkably sweet and – whisper it – nice. His lazy drawl is perfect for the "lonely in this world" lyric (even if he does go out of time halfway through). Wakeman's piano playing is a tad cumbersome, dragging the song back, and the lead guitar fills are much too intrusive, as they are throughout the album. Robinson seems to have no grasp of mixing. He's shamed by the skilful, deft, near-exemplary use of such guitar fills on the later *Coney Island Baby* album.

It's an unabashedly heterosexual lyric – the love of a good woman will see you right – something that must logically be put down to Bettye's influence, though it's important to remember that in early Lou Reed songs the narrator is rarely, if ever, Reed himself. At least, not consciously.

WALK AND TALK IT

"Hail hail rock and roll!" applauded one reviewer. "And hail Lou Reed for getting right back to the essence of what it's all about." "Walk And Talk It" crept out as a single in both the US and the UK, coupled with "Wild Child". The opening guitar riff is typically early '70s – i.e. not half as ballsy as it thinks it is – but infectious nonetheless in a kind of Keef Richards-Lite way. The girls' vocals again prop up Lou's tones: he's wonderfully, determinedly flat. He strains to make the trad phrases and parlance of rock his own, but ad-libs like "Young momma!" only emphasise how cool his own best couplets are: "I got refined carbon in my eyelids, dear" is nothing if not original.

Again, the drummer overplays, and the guitarists make it sound like the drummer is understated. Too many lead solos spoil what could've been a bewitching broth. One imagines John Cale hearing this track and wincing.

LISA SAYS

"His arresting lyrics combine a New York street punk sensibility and rock song clichés with a powerful poetic gift," reckoned *Rolling Stone*. "On 'Lisa Says', the lines, 'Lisa says hey baby if you stick your tongue in my ear/Then the scene around here will become very clear,' say as much about raw sex as any two lines I can think of in rock literature."

Though Reed at the time said the song was a tribute to Lisa Robinson, it's doubtful that even the swinging Richard Robinson was permitting "raw sex" between the pair. In fact it's just one in a proud tradition of Reed songs that employ a "she says" conceit: see also Candy, Caroline, Stephanie. From a subdued opening the track picks up a gear when the backing girls soar in: there's a feel that pre-empts *Transformer*, and Reed sings like someone who is effortlessly cool rather than someone trying hard to be effortlessly cool. After an effective false ending, the jaunty "Why am I so shy?" coda and contrived, camp "Such pretty eyes!" set piece are genuinely charming. In the third movement (if you will), Cattini leads a slower, bluesy groove. The original orphaned Velvets version, with equally strangled vocals, turned up later on *VU* and various compilations.

BERLIN

"I always wanted to do the Barbra Streisand thing, a real nightclub torch song… if you were Frank Sinatra, you'd loosen your tie, light a cigarette…"

"Afterhours", the last song Reed had played with the dying Velvets, cast him as a laconic, pensively smoking cabaret singer, intrigued by decadent Sally Bowles-style glamour. The supremely evocative "Berlin" took the idea further, but this sketchy realisation was only a blueprint for what was to become the starting point for his most ambitious album, 1973's magnum opus of the same name.

At heart it's not that different from the later version, though it includes a chorus, and a palatable if unnecessary rock-out fade. The accompaniment is surprisingly sympathetic, as if for a change the musos are listening to Reed's "unconventional" vocal

technique. Hearing his croaky croon here, you think already of "Perfect Day". There's a rich double-tracked guitar motif (a bit Yes, but a bit more like Mick Ronson's stock-in-trade, soon to be co-opted by Lou). Notoriously, the atmospheric lyric is here derailed at the climax by Lou's throwaway of "don't forget, hire a vet". He dropped it from all subsequent lyric sheets. He was quoting an American government slogan, the "vet" in question being a Vietnam veteran, not – as some Brits misinterpreted it – a doctor who attends to sick horses and poorly dogs. The confusion rather scuppered the song's melodramatic impact this time around.

I LOVE YOU

"I always wanted to write a song called 'I Love You' and make it fresh," Reed remarked. "If I could take a phrase like that and turn it into something, then that would be a real accomplishment." And he did. Perhaps because it's so against-type, this pastel-shaded acoustic number, all West Coast laid-back vibe as opposed to East Coast vitality, works on every level. For once the production is subtle, and Lou's voice even tackles a key change (well, almost). But the keen-eyed, cold-hearted, realist lyricist in him adds, after the proclamations of love, "right this minute" and "at least for now". Two and a quarter minutes of perfect judgement.

WILD CHILD

"I wonder," pondered Stephen Holden in *Rolling Stone*, "if anyone else could get away with, 'Oh can I break your heart'." Often likened to Dylan's "Bringing It All Back Home", this easy-to-like rocker fitted snugly and unobtrusively into later "Best Of" sets. It's a fine early example of Reed's knack for listing oddball characters and their idiosyncratic quirks, giving us a writerly glimpse of the Manhattan demimonde he'd thrown himself into in the Factory years. "I'm always studying people that I know," he'd said. Chuck, Bill, Ed and Lorraine – "always back to Lorraine"

– conduct their kinky affairs with pills, suicide, crack-ups, wine and, er, "sweet cheese". Lorraine appears to be the wild child – "and nobody can get at her". Meanwhile, Lou's Bettye calms down after her "auditions" make her ill. It's an excellent rangefinder for Lou's story-telling style, with the band forging a dynamic that supports his narrative edifice without demolishing the foundations.

LOVE MAKES YOU FEEL

It floats in like a Crosby, Stills, Nash and Young reverie but then puffs up its chest and hits a more elevated plateau. A small but flawlessly formed gem, with smart lyrics and sharp chords biding their time before the glorious payoff: "Love makes you feel ten foot tall… and it sounds like this!" The lovely fractious cascading rumble that follows that punch line was – in a matter of just a few seconds – highly influential on much '80s and '90s British indie music, from Orange Juice and Postcard to the Jesus And Mary Chain and My Bloody Valentine. It climbs down from the sky deftly too.

"It's a great deal of fun for me to do a lyric like that," remarked Lou. "People say, oh it's Lou Reed, it must be a put-on. Well, they're wrong. I love that stuff, always have, always will. It's hopeless, there's nothing to be done about it. I'll listen to that stuff till they put me away."

One could happily listen to this till they rattled over with the leg-irons. It really does catch the fleeting spirit of falling in love.

RIDE INTO THE SUN

A chugging riff, excessive and gratuitous lead-guitar interruptions, and Lou trying hard to sound effortlessly warm and inviting – yes, it's just another filler track, flopping through borderline comical production. Any frail beauty is stomped out by those look-at-me guitars, and just when you think one has shut up, another infuriatingly screams in. It's as if Robinson made a pact with the session men: do this, and I'll let you solo to your heart's content. All over the vocal sections? Sure, fine! Why not? Knock yourself out!

Compare and contrast with the Velvets' take. This one's memorable only for the line, "It's hard to live in the city", which has "recurring Lou Reed motif" written all over it.

OCEAN

Written as far back as 1968, and once demoed for *Loaded* with Cale, this reminded new listeners that there was more to Reed than vaguely subverted bubblegum. That he could do alienating art noise. Unfortunately this version's such a right royal mess that it alienates for all the wrong reasons. Reed was annoyed at how he could never get the song quite how he envisioned it, and booted up the wanton melodrama. Robinson's production must rank as one of the all-time farragoes, and Cattini's drums – or, at least, the way they're recorded – are an embarrassment. Cymbals, kettledrums and timpani (or approximations of same) whoosh across the speakers – they're supposed to sound like crashing waves, or perhaps the Velvets. They're just a mess. Wakeman wobbles through portentous piano. When Lou starts to shriek his words like a demented parrot you beg for Bowie to come along and give him singing lessons. Oceanic? Well, Robinson's certainly out of his depth. Is that final sound borrowed from The Gong Show? It should be.

"It evokes the ocean in an unfairly unpleasant manner," summarised Lou. Got that right. "A guy goes mad on the track, the ocean engulfs him. The person's just one example of a mad person … a lot of my friends are mad, but aren't we all? Who isn't? Especially in cities. My God."

Lou Reed was still learning the map as a solo performer. His city required a bold new architect, one who understood and appreciated his temperamental clay. In short, he needed to ride a new wave.

TRANSFORMER

November **(1972)**

VICIOUS ❧ ANDY'S CHEST ❧ **PERFECT DAY** ❧ HANGIN' ROUND ❧ **WALK ON THE WILD SIDE** ❧ MAKE UP ❧ **SATELLITE OF LOVE** ❧ WAGON WHEEL ❧ **NEW YORK TELEPHONE CONVERSATION** ❧ I'M SO FREE ❧ **GOODNIGHT LADIES** ❧ **Produced:** David Bowie and Mick Ronson **Recorded at:** Trident Studios, London **Musicians:** Lou Reed (vocals, guitars); Mick Ronson (guitars, string and bass arrangements, piano, recorders, backing vocals); David Bowie (backing vocals, arrangements); Klaus Voorman (bass); Herbie Flowers (bass, string bass, tuba, arrangement on "Goodnight Ladies"); John Halzey (drums); Barry DeSouza (drums); Ritchie Dharma (drums); Ronnie Ross (baritone sax); The Thunder Thighs (backing vocals).

The album that made Lou Reed a household name – at least in all the most disreputable households – *Transformer* was a transatlantic hit, and remains a timeless classic of palatable pop transgression. Masterminded by hottest rising superstar David Bowie and his often-undervalued sidekick Mick Ronson (fresh off the back of *Ziggy Stardust*), it brought Reed's songwriting and unique vocal stylings into the limelight that admirers like Bowie considered the New Yorker's due. It turned the cult of Reed into a religion, gave him a freak best-selling single, and dangerously inflated his confidence and ego: a mixed blessing. It also bestowed upon him a near-indelible degenerate image, with which he was to wage ambivalent war for years to come. And for all the seductive glam-rock smoke and mirrors and exquisite production, it's a group of great songs, infused with the nervy, needy spirit of Warhol, and delivered deadpan by a star whose moment had arrived.

Things were moving quickly for Reed now. Bowie, a fan, had been namechecking the Velvets and the Factory at every opportunity (the track "Andy Warhol" had graced *Hunky Dory*) and playing their songs in his live set since 1970, to the point where Reed was perhaps better known among music lovers in the UK than in the US. Bowie, calculatedly or disingenuously, touted his new American heroes – Reed and Iggy Pop – around London, introduced them to the press, and record companies queued up to fawn. If what Bowie saw in Iggy was the true rock'n'roll animal his own cerebral self wasn't, Lou arguably combined the best extremes of both. (The strange three-way friendship was much later alluded to in the fascinating if flawed Todd Haynes movie *Velvet Goldmine*).

Reed had always, always worn black with the Velvets, accustomed as he was to having films projected onto him. Bowie's wife Angie persuaded him to dress more exotically, and he threw himself into the challenge, adopting an alabaster-faced, black-eyeliner persona: The Phantom Of Rock. "I realised," he said, "that I could be anything I wanted." (Well, except for pretty, sure, Lou). On 8 July 1972 he made his debut on a London stage at the Royal Festival Hall as Bowie's special guest (at the height of Ziggymania), in a benefit show for Save The Whales. A week later he made his own sold-out solo debut, with the Tots, at the Kings Cross Cinema, liberally lacing his set with Velvets classics, pleased at the audience's knowledgeable response. Glammed up and swaggering, he had a new manager, Dennis Katz (savvy enough to nurture the Bowie connection). "I did three or four shows like that, then it was back to leather," was Reed's later, inaccurate disclaimer. "I was just kidding around. I'm not into make-up."

Bowie and Mick Ronson, along with top-of-the-range musicians and unsung engineer Ken Scott, ushered Reed into Trident Studios as early as August. The "bisexual revolution" was afoot. Sessions were often rushed, and not always cheery, as Bowie had other titanic commitments – his own Ziggy tour,

The mighty Mick Ronson

writing and recording with Mott The Hoople for "All The Young Dudes", promotion. It seems incredible in retrospect that he managed to make such a miracle of a rush-job like *Transformer*, and much credit must go to the versatile Ronson and the unflappable Scott. And once the honeymoon of hero worship had cooled, there were temperamental clashes, the read-about-it British leaning towards urbane elegance, the lived-it New Yorker Reed snapping their heads off with streetwise sarcasm and sometimes thuggish intimidatory tactics. But Reed had to admire Bowie's ideas, which were simultaneously musical and theatrical. Bowie encouraged Reed to bring forth more tales and mysteries from the Warhol years, the characters, the art. He wanted to hear about underground New York. Reed had a handful of songs he'd roughed out for a once-mooted, now-defunct project of a musical based on Nelson Algren's 1956 novel of vice and addiction, *A Walk On The Wild Side*: these waltzed into the mix. The work became a shiny yet suitably seedy celebration and exploration of the drive for love that sometimes takes a wrong turn into impersonal sex or imperfect drugs.

Creem magazine declared, "*Transformer* is what the third Velvet Underground album would have sounded like if David Bowie had been in production back then. There's something especially fine about it which sets it apart from all the other crappy platters being released lately. I mean, hell, at least it ain't anal-retentive." More astutely, Nick Kent in the *New Musical Express* decreed of "Walk On The Wild Side" – a bizarre British Top Ten hit, though not until six months later – "Any song that mentions oral sex, male prostitution, methedrine and valium, and still gets Radio One airplay, must be truly cool." He forgot to mention the sex change, but you take the point.

Reed conceded that the business people around him had urged him to work with Bowie, knowing he'd make a record both vital and viably commercial. "And it turned out to be totally true, didn't it?" There was, he added, much sexual ambiguity on the album, and "two outright gay songs, but carefully worded so that the straights can miss out on the implications and enjoy them without being offended". There was also Dada-ist wordplay and, in flashes, a sweet, more innocent brand of candour. Of Mick Rock's memorable sleeve, Reed pouted, "It has a cover you just won't believe. The back has a photo of a well-hung young stud looking into the mirror, and this sylph-like 40s female creature staring out at him. The front cover has the most beautiful face in the world. Mine."

The symbiotic relationship with Bowie was to wind up in tears, tantrums and fisticuffs, but for now they settled for damning each other's talents with faint praise. Reed eventually resented the kudos people gave to Bowie for "making" Reed, and was too narcissistic and bitter to take it with good grace. "He's very clever," he muttered. "We had a lot in common. He learned how to be hip. Associating with me brought his name out to a lot more people." To 99% of British record buyers, the opposite was true. "He's very good in the studio," the curmudgeon allowed. At other times, he's said, "I love David Bowie – the kid's got everything, everything," and, "There's only one person with a viler temper than mine, and that's Bowie." For his part, Bowie weighed in, with rather more of a grasp of dignity, with, "When he's not being troubled by things around him, Lou's a very generous person, with time and conversation." Everyone agreed Ronson was a prince. "He plays in exactly the style I want," nodded Reed. "Upfront."

With the album a definitive breakthrough success, Lou toured the States in early 1973. Slightly surreally, given the campery of his album, image and times, he then married Bettye Kronstadt. "When I get bored," he intoned, "funny things happen."

Although "Walk On The Wild Side" was one of the most ubiquitous and distinctive songs of its era, and he was now the solo star he'd always been too cool to admit he desperately wanted to be, he wasn't laughing for long.

VICIOUS

Directly inspired by Warhol, "Vicious" boasts one of the all-time simple-but-great rock'n'roll guitar riffs. Said Reed to journalist David Fricke years later, "Andy said, 'Why don't you write a song called "Vicious"?' And I said, 'Well, Andy, what kind of vicious?' 'Oh, you know, vicious like: I hit you with a flower.'" Ronson's playing – though arguably the guitars could have been recorded with a touch more whoomph – is tight and tough, going for broke á la Ziggy's "Moonage Daydream" over the fade. "It's a hate song," declared Reed. "The first album was all love songs; this one's all hate songs. I drink constantly," he told Lester Bangs over double Scotches. "I'm getting tired of liquor because there's just nothing strong enough."

In the mind's ear, "Vicious" always seems more savage than it is in reality, where, on an otherwise superbly produced album, it's misleadingly muddy and soft. We do, though, get the first blast of the pop-operatic backing vocals by Bowie and the female duo Thunder Thighs that will prove such an enlightening feature of *Transformer*. In one couplet, Lou gives us notice of the nursery-rhyme-from-purgatory themes to come on one of his wittiest albums: "Hey, why don't you swallow razor blades?/You must think I'm some kind of gay blade …"

Ziggy played guitar in radical fashion

ironic light-hearted, almost throwaway, feel. But Bowie and Ronson pulled back the tempo and squeezed forward all the lyrics' macabre, madcap melodrama. Bats, rattlesnakes, "bare bears" and bloodsuckers play their parts. Reed then added a new verse for this take: Daisy May's body mutates irrationally – her hands become her feet, her bellybutton becomes her mouth "which meant she tasted what she'd speak", and her nose reaches her toes, much amusing Lou to the point of a dodgy music-hall "How'd she smell? Terrible!" joke. "I don't know what it means either," he confessed. "I just put it in so people could hear it when they were stoned and laugh at it." The finale of "Swoop, swoop! Rock, rock!" is flush with the multiple-tracked vocals experimentation Bowie (and Ken Scott) was keen on at the time. Relishing a kind of post-modern mock doo-wop feel, it must have greatly appealed to the authentic doo-wop lover in Reed.

PERFECT DAY

And it's always tricky to guess at the "authenticity" or otherwise of emotion in the songs of this era. Is "Perfect Day" a transcendent, beautifully vulnerable love song, or a sneaky subversive paean to smack? Either way, to many this is Reed's crowning moment. Of course the picture's been clouded, or rather inflated beyond conventional discernment, by the somewhat surreal '90s success of the song when used as a BBC commercial, with famous faces from the hip to the hackneyed (from Bono to Boyzone to Pavarotti) queuing up to sing a line each. Many of them presumably had no idea what they were singing. And the vast majority of the record buyers who rocketed the subsequent single to Number One were of the demographic that'd likewise propel Beatles covers by Pop Idol contestants to the top of the charts. It's all very odd. With Reed, nothing's straightforward.

"Twenty-five years on, 'Perfect Day' became even bigger than 'Wild Side' ever was," Reed has chuckled recently. "Go figure."

Back in 1972, lovers of *Transformer* couldn't know of such future strangeness. While it seemed a tad

Eventually released as a single on both sides of the Atlantic, it failed to follow up the freak success of "Walk On The Wild Side", yet remains one of Reed's best-known songs.

ANDY'S CHEST

All about Warhol's shooting? "It's about that ... even though the lyrics don't sound like it," said Reed. Nothing so linear here as a serious examination of Lou's reaction to Valerie Solanas's deranged attempt upon Andy's life, but a lovely lilting tune full of inspired burlesque imagery. Some of it spoke to Andy, some to Valerie: most of it just enjoyed playing with words. He'd written it some years earlier, for the Velvets, and that band had recorded it in May 1969 with a suitably

someone more accustomed to being a curmudgeon than a loved-up cherub, it's a classic of casting against type. Someone else, someone good.

HANGIN' ROUND

Lou's on the more familiar ground of world-weary wit and snidey sarcasm on this straightforward rocker. Bowie and Ronson had bashed through Chuck Berry's "Round And Round" not long before, and here's one of the few places you can believe it. But as ever, Ronson makes the standard riffing zing and spark, and the chorus packs a mean enough punch.

The put-downs are prickly, curt and pinpoint, their cheeks blazing with camp yet caustic Ziggy attitude. The arrogant "You're still doing things that I gave up years ago" has entered common usage, and naturally we wonder who it's aimed at.

"I never mean what I say," Reed told one interviewer. "I never keep to things. I told some journalist I was very hung up on cowboys. If I saw him today, I'd probably tell him I was really aggressive and that all cowboys are a bunch of assholes. I'm really very inconsistent." That'll explain why "Kathy" is wearing "dentures clamped tightly to her nose", then.

WALK ON THE WILD SIDE

Whether he likes it or not, this – along with "Perfect Day" – is the song for which the world at large will remember Lou Reed. "It was just one of twelve songs," he recalled on the sleeve notes of his 2003 compilation *NYC Man*. "I didn't think any more of it than the other ones. I mean, the track that I really liked was 'Hangin' Round'. Which is why no one listens to me."

When hosting his remarkable, rambling 1978 shows at New York's Bottom Line (a punky cabaret set documented on the thrilling *Take No Prisoners* live album), Reed would tell the story of how he came to write the song. Working for his father in 1971, he reckoned, he'd been wooed by theatrical

obtuse to accept a Reed song as "romantic", possibly, just possibly, this one genuinely was. With its tale of lovers drinking sangria in the park, feeding animals in the zoo, catching a movie, it touched a nerve and *seemed* tender. "You just keep me hangin' on," with all due respect to the Supremes, was one poignant payoff; "You're going to reap just what you sow" was another. And the line which convinced most Reed diehards that this was a straightforward love song to Bettye was: "You made me forget myself/I thought I was someone else … someone good."

For all the overfamiliarity after the bombastic schmaltz of the BBC version, the understated yet still elegiac and epic original, with Ronson's swooning strings and piano lending grandeur, remains a thing of frail wonder. It captures not just the thrill and excitement of falling in love but the attendant hesitancy and fear that the blessed state can't last forever, and that there's not a damn thing you can do about it anyway. And with Reed's singing voice – of course – suggesting that these are the sentiments of entrepreneurs, keen to adapt a musical from Nelson Algren's book (described by *Time* magazine as "rich in shock"). "It's about cripples in the ghetto," drawled Reed. "Are you kidding? I'm the best qualified person to set music to a book about cripples?" Though the project never panned out, Lou pinched the title and played around with a song which bore references to obvious, time-honoured New York landmarks such as 42nd Street, the Empire State Building, etc. But the influence of Warhol, and then Bowie's enthusiasm for all things Andy, encouraged Reed to people the song with the New York characters he knew about and had been transfixed by: Candy Darling, Holly Woodlawn, Joe Dallesandro ("Little Joe") and Joseph Campbell ("the Sugar Plum Fairy"), all members (actors, artists, transvestites, cross-dressers, junkies, wannabes, whatever) of Warhol's pansexual "superstar" parade, were hereby both eulogised and then sent up by the song's ironic, taunting title.

"If I retire now," Reed said unguardedly, "'Walk On The Wild Side' is the one I'd want to be known by. That's my masterpiece. That's the one that'll make them forget 'Heroin'." It actually introduced Reed to an entirely fresh audience, who'd never even heard "Heroin".

Magically, Herbie Flowers' two-note bass slide and baritone sax from Ronnie Ross (Bowie's saxophone teacher) created an atmosphere to die for, somehow both swaggering and haughtily restrained. Soft acoustic guitars and brush drums allow Reed's narration to drip with presence. Then, of course, the "coloured girls" (beautifully faded in by Ken Scott) go "doo da doo" in one of the simplest yet most effective payoff hooks in pop's alternative history. New York was a place where Reed would continue to find rich lyrical pickings for the rest of his career, but if the (much) later *New York* album was more detailed, this is where he nailed it neatest, nastiest and best.

Radio DJs lapped it up, too dense to pick up on the sex-and-drugs references. Candy Darling all but roped Lou in to the idea of a Candy-Sings-Lou album, but sadly died of cancer in 1974. "I found the secret with that song," said Reed.

Rich in shock, indeed. It took seven months, however, to climb to No. 10 in the UK. It was an American hit, and, because of it, every confused teenager owned a shiny copy of *Transformer*. Reed, still in thrall to the preachings of Delmore Schwartz, may have anguished over "selling out" as a writer, but the strong likelihood is his solo career would have petered out in the early '70s without it. (Lisa and Richard Robinson, proving themselves to be small enough to be petty, were exercising their influence to get the album butchered by the American press. But *Transformer* developed a life of its own.) Instead, as it oozed and seeped from radios around the world, Reed now did his very best to implode of his own accord.

"Walk On The Wild Side" is purring malevolence, sarcasm so slick you want to stroke it.

On the sidelines, Andy Warhol had mixed feelings. On the one hand, Reed was milking mileage yet again from their association, which he resented. On the other hand, the song was ubiquitous, and was proving to be terrific publicity for his trilogy of films – *Flesh*, *Heat* and *Trash* – which starred Joe Dallesandro and a newly namechecked drag queen or two. Ticket sales to the films boomed. It seemed everyone felt the urge to take a walk on the wild side, even if only vicariously. Just doo da doo it.

MAKE UP

Possibly Reed's most unambiguous statement of homosexual sympathies. (By the time of *Transformer*'s 25th anniversary reissue, he'd become staunchly revisionist, denying any youthful "experimentation" to the point of nixing yours truly's commissioned (by the record company) sleeve

notes and replacing them with something that focused solely on the music and glossed over the lyrics' impact.) "We're coming out, out of our closets" was/is fairly difficult to misinterpret, if you ask me. It was the slogan the Gay Liberation movement had adopted as a global motto and rallying call at the time, and Reed supported it, though not to the uncompromising extent that, say, Bowie had in the UK during this period.

"The gay life at the moment isn't that great," he said in 1973. "I wanted to write a song which made it terrific, something you'd enjoy." Ironically, by painting the gay lifestyle as being all about lip gloss, eyeliner and perfume, he reinforced certain stereotypes, and his macho drawl on the track led many listeners to assume he was lampooning.

This day in the life of a transvestite is enhanced by Herbie Flowers' tuba obbligato.

SATELLITE OF LOVE

Another jewel, with a Bowie/Ronson arrangement redolent of "Drive-In Saturday" maximising its dynamic shifts and baroque appeal. The piano flourishes in all the right spots, and the backing vocals, finger clicks and handclaps are just beautiful, Bowie reaching stratospherically high over the coda, his voice(s) struggling to contain both angels and demons. Ken Scott has, on television documentaries, shown via the mixing desk that they could have done even more with this astonishing contribution if – contrary to popular myth – Bowie hadn't stressed that this album was about Lou, not him. Even Reed – not one to overpraise collaborators – has nodded his assent since the turn of the century. "I love Bowie's background vocals on his records, and I love them on this record. It's not the kind of part I could ever have come up with if you'd left me alone with a computer program for a year, but David hears those parts. Plus he's got a freaky voice and can go that high and do that. It's very, very beautiful, and he's a great singer."

But the song – a sweet melody in the process of being turned sour by jealousy and paranoia – is in itself a Reed classic (often covered since by, among others, U2 and Annie Lennox), which somehow managed to flop as a sure-thing single. It too had been demoed by the Velvets during the *Loaded* sessions, but surely not with this grace and grandeur.

If the middle eight concerns itself with the obscure object of desire being "bold" with "Harry, Mark and John", the song's main thrust seems to express a comatose wonderment at and with technology. "I watched it for a little while/I like to watch things on TV" succeeds in both hinting at Warhol's I-am-a-machine passivity and calling to mind Bowie's subsequent telly-entranced phases as Thomas Jerome Newton in Nicolas Roeg's film *The Man Who Fell To Earth*. Addiction can take many forms.

WAGON WHEEL

A generic guitar chugger, its intro faintly pre-empting Mott The Hoople frontman Ian Hunter's later "Once Bitten, Twice Shy". Nothing exceptional in itself, it breezes by on both the goodwill generated by the outstanding songs around it, and on another durably impressive production job. "If you get kicks from danger/Just kick her in the head and rearrange her," sneers Reed's less sensitive side with marvellous callousness.

A sinister bass throb breaks up the riffing, and the mock-religious spell ("Oh, heavenly father, what can I do …") has the whiff of Bowie and Ronson wondering how they can jazz up a run-of-the-mill rock piece. Yet for all its inability to go to new places, "Wagon Wheel" is exactly where Reed had been trying to get to since the Velvets' demise. In the context of *Transformer* it's weak, but in the wider context of Reed's transition to a solo star, it's an indication of how Bowie and Ronson were, in terms of musical invention, pulling him up by the bootstraps. Again, whether he appreciated it or not.

NEW YORK TELEPHONE CONVERSATION

A genuine oddity and, at a minute and a half, full of quirky charm. Reed and Bowie duet (complete with catty, hissy whispers) on a gossipy send-up of Warhol's lonely daily telephone life (as documented in vastly more detail in the pop artist's bitchy and hugely entertaining books *POPism* and *Diaries*). Could the sigh of "Oh, how sad" and the plea of "What shall we wear?" possibly *be* more camp? Did Tim Curry play this before getting into his role as Frank N. Furter in *The Rocky Horror Picture Show*?

"Did you hear who did what to whom?" is (im)pure Warhol, encapsulating both the man's shy reclusiveness and his love of glitzy shallow party gatherings. As with all matters Warhol, and indeed all matters Reed, the paradox is inherent.

I'M SO FREE

Like "Wagon Wheel", an unexceptional pop-rock work-out in itself, but, sailing on the spirit of the album, a blast. Those handclaps are nicely loose, just a fraction off, and again the interplay between the buoyant backing vocals and Reed's rough tones is crucial. More meaningless, doped-out animal references – "Do you remember the shape I was in?/I had horns and fins" – and Ronson having fun over the fade. The chasm in quality and taste between Ronson's guitars on this album and those of the various axe heroes on the previous album is immeasurable. Reed may never have been a prime candidate to be cited "mother nature's son", but everything he claimed on this album was coming up trumps, and all the underground iconic imagery he'd been selling for years was now being unilaterally lapped up. "A lot of it reminded me of when I was with Warhol; it was just that a lot more people were doing it," opined Reed of the glam era. "Then it became very stylised and commercial. And when that happened, it became nothing."

"We had really good fun on the *Transformer* sessions," he admitted, with the serenity of hindsight, as lately as 2003. "Great studio, great engineer. Both Bowie and Ronson ran things, got the musicians, I didn't have to worry about any of that. It's always fun to work with people who have a lot of ideas. David has lots and lots. Mick was a great arranger. You couldn't go wrong."

GOODNIGHT LADIES

Famously arranged and played by "Herbie Flowers and some of his friends", the farewell track on *Transformer* is the last thing you expect. A tuba-led, Sunday lunchtime old-style jazz piece, the antithesis of the Velvet Underground, and somehow it works. Flowers invents another bizarre backdrop over which Reed can intone his shards of cynicism. Lou actually sounds like he's having a good time over this barroom lullaby, jaded and jaundiced as ever but crooning so enthusiastically he stretches "tequila" into (at least) five syllables. Sometimes he sounds more Leonard Cohen than Cohen, as he again bemoans a disappointing love life, and the notion that he's eating TV dinners and gazing at the anaesthetic of the small screen on a "lonely Saturday night".

It has a hint of the stage musical about it, albeit in a boozed-up way. As if Reed's mind's eye was watching its own nocturnal cabaret. It turned out that was exactly the nightmare he was dreaming up, and just as America followed Britain's example by consuming the treasure of *Transformer*, just as Reed had found the ideal pioneering-pop arrangements for his vignettes of sickly city life, he (temporarily) pensioned off the Phantom Of Rock persona and elected to "totally destroy them. This one will show them I'm not kidding." He was about to take a massive gamble – a gamble that backfired commercially but was a creative masterstroke. At the time, everyone hated it with a passion. In retrospect, it was a bull-headed burst of serious genius. "It" was the holy horror of *Berlin*.

BERLIN

October **(1973)**

BERLIN ❧ LADY DAY **❧ MEN OF GOOD FORTUNE ❧ CAROLINE SAYS 1 ❧ HOW DO YOU THINK IT FEELS ❧ OH, JIM ❧** CAROLINE SAYS 2 **❧ THE KIDS ❧** THE BED **❧ SAD SONG ❧ Produced:** Bob Ezrin **Recorded at:** Morgan Studios, London (overdubs in London and New York) **Musicians:** Michael Brecker (tenor sax); Randy Brecker (trumpet); Jack Bruce (bass – except "Lady Day" and "The Kids"); Aynsley Dunbar (drums – except "Lady Day" and "The Kids"); Bob Ezrin (piano, mellotron); Steve Hunter (electric guitar); Tony Levin (bass on "The Kids"); Allan Macmillan (piano on "Berlin"); Gene Martynec (acoustic guitar, synth, vocal arrangements, bass on "Lady Day"); Jon Pierson (bass trombone); Lou Reed (vocals, acoustic guitar); Dick Wagner (electric guitar, background vocals); Blue Weaver (piano on "Men Of Good Fortune"); B.J. Wilson (drums on "Lady Day" and "The Kids"); Steve Winwood (organ, harmonium); plus The Choir (Bob Ezrin, Dennis Ferrante, Steve Hyden, Elizabeth March, Lou Reed, Dick Wagner).

Everybody said, 'Don't do it Lou, you're asking for it.' So we did it. And the results have been very strange."

In the tinsel-hearted taboo-busting early '70s, it appears, the one thing you weren't encouraged to do was depress the hell out of everyone. It seems almost quaint now that Lou Reed's magnum opus was so controversial, provoking extraordinary quantities of vitriol and bile from those expecting the "sensible" career move of a frolicsome follow-up to "Walk On The Wild Side". The list of artists who've made careers out of exploiting their own darker mood swings since (from the anger of punk through Morrissey and Cobain to Morrisette and Tindersticks) would fill pages. Reed even had leavening dry humour within the lines of *Berlin* – not that many noticed. It does, however, remain definitive: as a dubious honour it regularly makes the top in any sniggering poll of Albums To Commit Suicide To. And if you were an impressionable young teen when it came out, already enamoured of *Transformer*, you were stunned, stirred and haunted by its *Grand Guignol* flourishes and ghostly pallor.

Reed was confused, elated, bewildered and freaked out by his sudden elevation to the role of America's Answer to Glam. He'd swung with the bright young rebels of London, and in New York that made him cool (much as the inverse is true: to this day, London lies down and laps up any band who've even so much as passed through

Manhattan on a shopping trip). When he began his early 1973 tour in New York, posters on subways blared, "Will you still be underground when Lou Reed surfaces?" The tour – again, perhaps unwisely, with the Tots – was to be mentally and physically gruelling for Reed, with much deliberate self-abuse and excess. He not only talked the talk, he walked the walk, wild as you like. He came close to destroying himself. Surreally, the icon of perversity chose this moment to marry the long-suffering (there were rumours that he beat her up) Bettye Kronstadt. Not entirely unpredictably, after some months of Reed ignobly assassinating her character to the press, they were divorced by the autumn. She may – not that it'd be a consolation to the poor woman – have been the muse for *Berlin*, as may Nico: we'll debate these possibilities shortly.

Freshly frazzled from an on-the-road blend of hedonism and masochism, his ego loving the attention and revving into overdrive, Reed re-entered the Willesden studio where he'd ill-advisedly recorded his first solo album (which had featured the original sketch of the ironic torch song "Berlin"), and dug in to write his first great American novel. Or rather, as Bob Ezrin put it, "a film for the ears".

Ezrin was young, keen, and high on his recent successes producing the band Alice Cooper, who he'd rocketed from deviant outsiders to cartoon rock

gods topping the charts. "Alice doesn't make it as a drag queen," sulked Lou. "He's just so ugly." Ezrin's patented guitar sound – heavy enough for the hard rockers, sweet enough for the charts – was much in demand. He was to go on to fine work with, among others, Pink Floyd and Jane's Addiction. But working with Reed on *Berlin* nearly destroyed his mind.

His devotion to the album was at least as fevered, if not more so, than Reed's. The "movie in music" idea was primarily his, and he assembled a then top-of-the-range squad of musicians, from big names like Jack Bruce and Steve Winwood to the hotter-than-hot session guitarists who'd fired up the Alice records – Steve Hunter and Dick Wagner. Reed's manager Dennis Katz pitched the record as a "black comedy": in truth it was so heavy on the black, and light on the comedy, that the sessions proved tortuous and rattling for all concerned. When it was eventually finished, Ezrin, his nerves shot, infamously told Reed that "the best idea is we put it in a box, put the box in a closet, leave it there and never listen to it again." The movie they'd made wasn't *Cabaret*, and it sure wasn't *The Sound Of Music*. It was an exorcism, an uncompromising journey into the heart of darkness. "We killed ourselves psychologically on that record," Reed has admitted. "We went so far into it that it was kind of hard to get out."

It prompted such a peculiar reaction that the reviews bordered on hysteria. "Probably the most depressing album of the decades," wrote *Sounds*. *Rolling Stone*, having previously tipped it to be "the Sergeant Pepper of the Seventies", in fact first printed a panning, then backed down and published a counter-review singing its praises, in a kind of oh-I-get-it-now volte-face. If *Transformer* had dressed up its tales of the dysfunctional in satin and lace, *Berlin* showed the night after the morning after. Loosely the narrative of a crumbling *ménage á trois* in an equally unsettled Berlin, it dealt with anxiety, obsessive jealousy, domestic (and other) violence, speed jags, a bad mother forsaking lost children, and suicide. And around all this, a veil of chilling, apathetic seen-it-all ennui, expressed by Reed's never-more-effective monotone. The music was vastly ambitious, a monument to the baroque, which began as claustrophobic rock and developed into spectacularly bleak cod-opera. The lyrics were fearless, misanthropic, misogynistic and confessional… or was Reed just making a point about how desensitised one could become when in the grasp of selfish extremes? For all his poses at playing the detached observer, it'd be naïve to whitewash him here. Some of himself dripped clammily through *Berlin*, and its imposing walls run with tears.

Berlin was a symbol for Reed. "It could be New York, too. It's just very straightforward and real. The lyrics are very direct and to the point. It's a realistic story… Berlin's a divided city, and a lot of potentially violent things go on there. And it just seemed better than calling it Omaha."

"It's involved with violence," he added later. "Both mental and physical. It takes place for real in Berlin in 1973. The really important thing is the relationship between the two major characters. The narrator is filling you in from his point of view, and his point of view is not particularly pleasant."

So who was the inspiration for the doomed principal character of "Caroline"? To some extent it must have been Bettye, Mrs Reed, whose marriage was not blossoming. Indeed, she attempted suicide herself soon afterwards, though it was kept hushed-up at the time. Lou wasn't, however, being covert or respectful. "During the recording sessions," he said five years later in an astonishingly candid interview with Allan Jones for *Melody Maker*, "my old lady – who was an asshole but I needed a female asshole to bolster me up, I needed a sycophant who could bounce around and she fit the bill, but she called it love, ha! – she tried to commit suicide in the bathtub at the hotel. Cut her wrists. She lived. But

we had to have a roadie with her there from then on." Upon the album's completion, taking off for a show in Paris, Reed booted her out of his entourage. Just like that.

Many theorists press the case that Nico was the muse. Reed had told one interviewer that while this wasn't a party album, not "something you enjoy", he'd disagreed with Nico when she'd asked him why he was encouraging suicide. "She didn't understand a word of it." The Germanic links obviously refuse to let the Nico-related readings fade away, and there was still a strange love-hate relationship between the former Velvet Underground colleagues. Also muddying the waters was the hanging-in-the-air suicide in September 1972 of the sadly deluded Andrea Feldman, aka Andrea Whips, a Factory crowd hanger-on who'd starred in the film *Heat*. She'd been declaring that she was herself Warhol. And also that Warhol was controlling her every action. If nothing else, this

plethora of sad stories would've persuaded Reed there was nothing too sensationalist about ending a "film for the ears" with a suicide.

Critics slated his lack of feeling. The irony is *Berlin* rumbles with more feelings than all but a handful of rock records ever made. Its drugginess, its aggression, its passivity – they're all about neediness.

"I don't have a clue where the inspiration came from," Reed shrugged to Nick Johnstone of *Uncut* in 2000. He recounted that he and Ezrin had fired each other up. "We had a little plot going on there. Boy meets girl, boy gets girl, boy loses girl, and that's when it ends." They agreed there was to be no happy ending. "I figured: cos that's not happening to me, how about you, Bob." Reed credited Ezrin with bringing in the musicians and arrangements, then added, "It was an amazing album. But a bitch. It caused grief for both of us. It had repercussions. Sometimes you do these things, and they're alive, they don't just sit there. They reverberate through your own personal life."

While the *New York Times* decreed it "one of the strongest, most original rock records in years", the first *Rolling Stone* piece (before the embarrassing retraction) growled, "There are certain records so patently offensive that one wishes to take some kind of physical vengeance on the perpetrators. His last shot at a once-promising career." Undoubtedly the venom of the American press had been concentrated by the spite of the Robinsons, and slowly some balance poked through. In Britain, for all its lack of populist hooks, the album rose to No. 7 (Reed never went higher until 1992's *Magic And Loss*). It didn't stick around the charts half as long as *Transformer* though. "The way that album was overlooked was probably the biggest disappointment I ever faced," he told Allan Jones, revealingly. "I pulled the blinds shut at that point. And they're remained closed."

Reed, stung and dejected and now drowning in drink and drugs, went into retreat or reinvention mode, stepping into the uniform his newer, less subtle fans wanted him to wear – that of the amped-up, speed-guzzling heavy-rock junkie. Cynical, defensive, whatever – it brought him popularity and album sales again. Although he's made many monumental and many mediocre records since, he's never constructed a monolith like the brave, bruising and curiously beautiful *Berlin*.

BERLIN

"I had to do *Berlin*. If I hadn't, I'd have gone crazy. If I hadn't got it out of my hair, I'd have exploded. It was a very painful album to make," Reed told Nick Kent. "I don't want to have to go through it again, having to say those words over and over."

According to one participant, keyboardist Blue Weaver, Reed didn't have to go through much, and there was reason he had to say the words repeatedly. "He can't do it straight," said Weaver in Peter Doggett's Reed biography *Growing Up In Public*. "He's got to go down to the bar and have a snort of this and that, and then they'd prop him up in a chair and let him start singing." Reed has denied the validity of Weaver's view, especially as he'd added, "We went in and laid down the instrumental tracks; the whole thing was done and sounded great. Then they brought Lou in …"

Ezrin's contribution is undeniable however: the album ebbs and flows with barely contained melodrama. Reed had felt threatened by Bowie's talent, but clicked with Ezrin. If the album's first half (originally, of course, Side One) has no blatantly consistent themes, lyrically or musically, apart from a pervasive gutsy gloom, Side Two is a (bitter) suite, four songs which travel like an epic poem from angst to agony to a burned-out apathy that rings louder than any depression.

The opening track is an intentionally pale reflection of the same source material on Reed's solo debut. There's something eerie about it: at once you know that this album, though it may be an emotional roller coaster, will not be a fun romp.

Nico: a muse for Berlin?

LADY DAY

Billie Holiday, the legendary jazz chanteuse, had a tragic life. She died of drugs and drink in 1959. The diva in Reed clearly related. While the female protagonist in all the songs on *Berlin* can be perceived as "Caroline", or aspects of her, some of the phrases in "Lady Day" do seem to be directly inspired by Holiday, whose nickname gives us the title. Reed gives us two snapshots – she enters the bar, unable to resist singing, and on the other side of the chorus "after the applause had died down", she climbs down off the bar and staggers home to her seedy hotel with its "greenish walls; a bathroom in the hall". The poignancy (and her booze/smack problems) is left to us to discern. We fill in the dots, knowing the truth. Reed's skill as a storyteller, throughout *Berlin*, has come on in leaps and bounds. While there are occasional howlers, and the narrative doesn't begin to hang together until almost halfway through, his literary influences are evident. He's learning to leave things out as well as add them. Part of *Berlin*'s greatness is what it implicitly suggests.

Which isn't to say it's as a rule restrained. Ezrin's already working wonders here, forming bombastic bridges and shapes, making each break from verse to chorus or back a major operation. He's a hungry young producer at the peak of his powers of invention, and though he's wonderfully pretentious, and can make a simple chord portentous, he's rarely pompous.

MEN OF GOOD FORTUNE

Hunter and Wagner's duelling guitars begin to hit their stride (they'll really break cover on "How Do You Think It Feels"); the pianos melt with melancholy. But hey, we're still relatively upbeat at this stage. The killer comes when Reed, having stared at the differing luck or energies of men from rich or poor backgrounds, shrugs impartially, "But me, I just don't care at all." It's a chilling foreshadowing of the way he (or "the narrator") will react to the tragic finale.

The rich, calculates Reed, have opportunities ("it takes money to make money, they say") that the poor don't. But on the other hand, the poor possess greater hunger and drive ("and to get it they'll die"). It balances out: swings and roundabouts. That Lou Reed himself actually had, somewhere in the background, a "rich daddy to fall back on", only gives the song an additional piquancy.

CAROLINE SAYS 1

Lisa, Stephanie, Candy. And now Caroline. Reed liked the "she says" format. Part one doesn't paint a warm picture of either heroine or narrator. She emasculates him, puts him down – "she wants a man, not just a boy" – but her taunts only seem to fan his ardour. For now. "She can't help but be mean, or cruel.../ At first I thought I could take it all..." There's then a clunkingly dreadful piece of poetry: "Just like poison in a vial, she was often very vile." We get the point, but the wordplay is weak as water. Then of course there's the telltale "she's still a German queen" (which Reed, contradicting every lyric printing he's approved over decades, pronounces as "Germanic"). Many are they who've decided this refers to Nico. The most likely and intelligent interpretation is that Caroline is a composite of all the women who'd fuelled Reed's misogyny. It manifests itself as a fevered brew of vulnerability, paranoia, suffering and bullying.

As on every track, Ezrin is doing plenty, fretting his fingers to the bone to make Reed's glider fly. When he ultimately returned to the States after the sessions, he underwent a breakdown. Well, Lou has that effect on lots of people, but Ezrin confessed, "It was a heroin rebound... a chemical breakdown. I'd rather have had a nervous breakdown. I hadn't known what heroin was till I went to England on this gig! We were all seriously ill. It took me a long time to get on my feet. I paid a heavy price. It put me out of commission for quite a while."

HOW DO YOU THINK IT FEELS

It's often hard to divine where Reed's autobiographical lines end and his objective storytelling tropes begin. It'd been the case with the Velvets; it was the case now. It's nurtured the mythology around him, yet he usually snarls that all his songs are stories, that he's a writer not a diarist. "How Do You Think It Feels" is so viciously, brilliantly sung and phrased that it's hard to believe it's not coming from his gnarly heart. His voice is urgent and desperate, yet weathered.

He asks his questions like pleas for clemency, for a reprieve from the existence he finds himself enduring. He's "speeding and lonely", "been up for five days" as he's "afraid of sleeping". The grunt of "come down here mama", seemingly apropos of nothing, is filthy with lust. But, in the perennial cry of the drug addict who has overindulged: "How do you think it feels to always make love by proxy?"

The guitars squeal and grind, dirtily, deliciously. Hunter and Wagner were landing a gig here. Patterns equally intense can be heard on Alice Cooper's *Billion Dollar Babies* album. Ezrin always ensures each flourish counts, means something dynamically (how far we've come since the first album!) and makes its point. For all the despair, the music's exhilarating, borderline euphoric. Finally, gasping, the singer croaks, "When do you think it stops?" He'd come down if he wasn't so low.

OH, JIM

A hush descends, then sullen rhythmic tom-tom drums rumble in. Any guitar/keyboard fills from here on in are answerable to that dogged, sinister rhythm. The mood has shifted. Now the drugs, the jealousy and the violence aren't exhilarating, not even in flashes. Forget trying to work out the plot line, however: this doesn't gel with *Berlin*'s "story". Reed is speaking to a man whose "two-bit friends" have pumped him full of pills and hate. His women troubles are just a bonus. Our narrator bestows the benefit of his wisdom upon him: "Beat her black and blue and get it straight." Ah, hitting the women – a solution that's commended more than once throughout the prickly, candid-to-a-fault, politically incorrect theatre that is *Berlin*.

We'll never know what was really going on in Reed's disastrous first marriage. And we'll never know for sure what the Reed–Nico rapport was like behind closed doors. We can hazard wildly irresponsible guesses though.

Jim's not going to find happiness in a hurry; neither is he going to bring it to others. Is there a touch of Reed himself in Jim? Is Reed bitching about his new-found crossover celebrity, and about Bowie, when he snaps, "All your two-bit friends, they asked you for your autograph/They put you on the stage, they thought it'd be good for a laugh." The album's like a hall of mirrors, with perspectives constantly shifting. If it was a film, you would be arguing about it for days afterwards.

CAROLINE SAYS 2

What used to be known as Side Two begins. Act Two, perhaps. For the next quarter of an hour, everything unravels, and few records in rock's history have engaged so furiously, if you're tough enough to hang with it. It pushes the envelope. Its emotional impact is harrowing, huge. This "Caroline Says" borrows a melody, and even some snatches of lyrics, from another Velvets' outtake, "Stephanie Says" (a version of which showed up on 1985's *VU*). "As she gets up off the floor", Caroline asks a man (possibly Jim) why he beats her – "it isn't any fun". She's "not afraid to die". With incredibly daring irony, the musical accompaniment is pretty.

She takes more drugs; her friends – "two-bit", presumably – just laugh. They call her "Alaska", probably because this rhymes conveniently with "ask her", although it does in fairness work as an extra constituent of the all-conquering cold of the atmosphere. And then, in a move any theatre director would be proud of, she puts her fist through

a windowpane. In a butter-wouldn't-melt voice, Reed, malicious more than mischievous, deadpans, "It was such a funny feeling."

There are show stoppers and there are show stoppers, and "Caroline Says 2" is phenomenal. Thing is, this show isn't stopping yet. In fact it's just getting... warmed up? No, no warmth here. Warmth is a discarded concept. What's happening with this album is its blood is just starting to freeze.

THE KIDS

For many listeners, "The Kids" is just too much. It goes too far. If only the fusion of words and music crossed the traditional boundaries, as this brazenly yet delicately does, more often. The voice, by now shell-shocked, the definition of ennui, tells of Caroline's further descent into personal hell. He's no help, he's "a tired man, no words to say", as Caroline becomes a jaded junkie-whore. The authorities are taking her children away, because "they said she was not a good mother". The list of men Caroline's being "unfaithful" with is extraordinary, seemingly listing the narrator's pet hates: "the black Air Force sergeant", "the Welshman from India"... To him, now, she's a "miserable rotten slut". And boy, does Reed spit it out like he means it.

As the elegiac chords rise and Reed fades away, the crying and wailing of young children rises to the foreground. There is no sound so grating as that of someone else's kids bawling and screaming: in this context, it's almost unbearable. And yet it makes the eight-minute track a thing of incomparably rare power, at least as daring as the Velvets' most experimental work-outs.

There's more: as the legend goes, the kids used were Bob Ezrin's. To make them appropriately distressed, while taping, he'd told them their mother wasn't coming back... ever again. Now that's putting art before family. When this anecdote (apocryphal or otherwise) got out, it backfired, and critics — who suddenly, overnight become apparent bastions of right-thinking conservative family values – used it as an example of how Reed and Ezrin had made an album that exploited misery and prostituted innocence.

Being music critics, one supposes that, having vented their spleen, they then returned to their green salads and peppermint tea.

Even Reed said, "It wasn't my idea to put actual children's voices crying there, but look at the effect of it. People have said to me, 'Oh Lou, that's too heavy-handed.' But some of them have said it while crying. It's distinctly unpleasant, no matter which way you look at it." In another interview, he mused, "Adults like the album, younger people have trouble relating to it. Women, and especially women who are mothers, get enormously depressed, but they like it. I think Bobby Ezrin was right when he said we should put it in a box and leave it there. But now it's out, and it's there, and people have to cope with it."

THE BED

And now the camera pans over to the bed, where Caroline laid her head at night, where "our children were conceived", and where, ultimately, "she cut her wrists, that odd and fateful night". Reed once suggested Bowie had written "Rock And Roll Suicide" for him: now, in an ongoing to-and-fro rivalry, he'd surpassed it. He's revisited the song in many live contexts since.

"My albums have continuously gotten seriously panned, and then twenty years later they're re-released and they say, 'This is a classic'."

For all the over-the-top aspects, "The Bed" contains some sublime poetry. Of the couple's ill-fated abode, the man states, "I paid for it with love and blood." He adds as an afterthought, "And these are the boxes that she kept on the shelf, filled with her poetry and stuff."

There's a cute, spooky-naïve refrain of "oh, oh, oh, what a feeling", but the atmosphere is all, and the narrator's stunned numbness is thoroughly credible. He's "not at all sad", he claims, but even Reed's rugged voice can't deadpan his way out of this one. He's feeling it.

SAD SONG

Perhaps *Berlin* is easier to empathise with if you think of its death motif as representing the death of love, the extinguishing of a once-brightly-blazing relationship that held great hope. Surely we've all been there. As each affair dies, as each promising romance fizzles out, we die a little. Another angle on *le petit mort*. Something in our hearts gives up the ghost, and our hearts become smaller. *Berlin* is about the death of innocence, and it really captures something.

The swansong, "Sad Song", is borderline bombastic, but what's led up to it has more than earned it. Among what seems to be several thousand musicians and a heavily populated choir (one can assume that by now Ezrin's obsession was reaching megalomaniac all-or-nothing proportions) the Brecker Brothers' sax and trumpet add an unusual waft of nostalgia.

Reed is muted, forlorn, which contrasts with the epic backdrop perfectly. And if this movie threatens to slip into Hollywood sentiment as, in the aftermath of Caroline's suicide, he gazes wistfully at his old photo album – "she looks like Mary, Queen of Scots" is an amazingly intimate, believable line – the cold-eyed writer in Reed soon snaps back, with "just goes to show how wrong you can be". The chorus says it like it is, undressed: "sad song, sad song". He concludes philosophically, "I'm gonna stop wastin' my time – somebody else would've broken both of her arms."

Brutal. Uncompromising. Savage. Tragic. There had never been, and has never been, another album like *Berlin*: not from Lou Reed, not from anybody. No wonder all concerned had to step away for a while once it was done. Lou himself chose to stride further and further off the rails,

ROCK 'N' ROLL ANIMAL
February **(1974)**

INTRO ❥ SWEET JANE ❥ **HEROIN** ❥ WHITE LIGHT/WHITE HEAT ❥ **LADY DAY** ❥ ROCK AND ROLL ❥ **Produced:** Steve Katz **Recorded at:** Academy Of Music, New York

A notorious live album, made by a virtual zombie. "*Rock'n'Roll Animal* was me revisiting the Velvets, thinking – maybe they'll catch on this time around."

Our focus in this book being on the best studio albums, and this being an unavoidably subjective reading, we can only touch briefly on the live albums. There have been plenty, probably too many: *Rock'n'Roll Animal* remains the most fabled.

For once, Reed made a "good" career move. Frustrated by the perceived failure of *Berlin*, freshly divorced from Bettye, he decided (and was persuaded by some of those around him) to play safe. To bang out his considerable catalogue of songs and shunt them from cult favourites to heavy crowd pleasers. Lou's idea of playing safe, however, incorporated great swathes of self-destruction along the way. Sensing that his fans wanted a freak show, he delivered, turning himself into a twitching, glaring monster. "They wanted to see me die," he suggested.

Snorting speed by the bucketful throughout the tour, but knowing he'd promised RCA a commercial record (or two) to "make up" for *Berlin*, he was pointed in a potentially valid direction by Steve Katz, brother of his manager Dennis. Steve Katz was unhappy as guitarist in Blood, Sweat And Tears, but Reed liked his playing style and brought him in to produce. Katz, despite being as sorry as Reed to see *Berlin* bomb, advised him to sacrifice some of his long-held mystique and get his old songs across to the new audience who'd come in on "Walk On The Wild Side". The band, including guitarists Hunter and Wagner, was, everyone agreed, "hot". Every song was belted out as a grinding riff, and Reed onstage did his sometimes-tragicomic best to mimic everyone from Jagger to Bowie to Iggy. Yes, thought Lou, this could work. To

a degree he was happy to shy away from where *Berlin* had taken him, and to distract himself from the sense of hopeless rejection he'd experienced when it wasn't universally acclaimed as a work of visionary genius.

The show at Howard Stein's Academy Of Music in New York in late December was a near riot. "Manic," recalled Lou. He and the Katz brothers quickly mixed the tapes, and proudly emerged with the fire-breathing beast that was *Rock'n'Roll Animal*. The band jam sans Reed, before he swaggers on for "Sweet Jane" and a ferocious focus on his Velvets material. Reviews were good, relieved almost, although *Rolling Stone* reckoned, "This is a record to be played loud. Faggots, junkies and sadists are not very pleasant, but theirs are the sensibilities Reed draws upon. His songs offer little hope. Nothing changes, nothing gets better." On the other hand, Robert Christgau wrote, "This is a live album with a reason for living." Its success on the US charts restored Reed's self-confidence, but simultaneously frazzled his mercurial ego. He would always maintain though that, "What I really liked was *Berlin*. *Rock'n'Roll Animal*, what a degrading thing that was."

He loved the live band, especially Hunter and Wagner, who brook little restraint here. Reed reported that he'd have liked to have included more *Berlin* songs, but "in the end we only used 'Lady Day' because we put on a fourteen-minute version of 'Heroin'." He pushed the album as a "clarification". He'd had his hit single, he shrugged, and now he wanted the younger generation to know what came before that. If he thought he was honouring the Velvet Underground's legacy, John Cale was less impressed.

"He thinks that by sticking to his guns he'll

succeed," said Cale, "and he has. He's got the whole sickness market tied up." Another time, Cale conceded, "I'm amazed at how different Lou and I were in our ideas now that I hear everything he's done since that time. It all just sounds like weak representations of tunes and nothing more. I mean, some of his songs in the Velvets really made a point. Now he just appears to be going round in circles, singing about transvestites and the like."

Chrissie Hynde, later the soulful and sassy singer/songwriter of the Pretenders, vividly reviewed the album in *NME*. "He looks like a monkey on a chain, court geek. Listen to him scramble to a corner, damaged and grotesque, huddled in rodent terror. Animal Lou. Lashing out in a way that could make the current S&M trend freeze in its shallow tracks. And the audience cheers after every song: we're with you, yeah, we always loved those songs, ha ha. Well... he hates you."

"It's the way those songs should be done... correctly," grizzled Reed.

Reed was throwing himself into his animal role, bashing his head against the bars of his imagined cage. Pale, paranoid, obviously ill, he appeared one day with what he said were Maltese crosses shaved into the sides of his head. Dennis Katz's objections to the "Nazi" image for once held sway, and Reed backed down. But while people could get him to (slightly) dilute his poses, they couldn't water down the frightening reality. He was losing his grip on the world around him.

SALLY CAN'T DANCE

August (us)
September (uk) **(1974)**

RIDE SALLY RIDE ➤ **ANIMAL LANGUAGE** ➤ BABY FACE ➤ **N.Y. STARS** ➤ KILL YOUR SONS ➤ **ENNUI** ➤ SALLY CAN'T DANCE ➤ **BILLY** ➤ **Produced:** Steve Katz and Lou Reed **Recorded at**: Electric Lady, New York **Musicians:** Lou Reed (vocals); Steve Katz (guitars); Danny Weiss (guitars); Prakash John (bass); Michael Fonfara (keyboards); Richard Dharma (drums); Pennti Glan (drums).

The heavy-metal Godzilla of *Rock'n'Roll Animal* having ripped the doors off, *Sally Can't Dance* shimmied through the gap and – heavily promoted – gave Reed his first (and only) US Top Ten album. Reed soon disowned it ("I hate that album, I despise that record") and biographer Peter Doggett has written, "It was – probably still is – the bottom of the pit." Yet for those of us who think Lou's later career has never matched his '70s heyday, it's a thing of wry beauty, humour and horror. Of course Lou, ever contradicting himself, is also on record as saying, "I like these songs a lot. I think they're the best I ever did."

Reed's first solo effort recorded outside England, it's one of the whitest ever "soul" albums – or, at least, its sleazy rock'n'roll exhibits some vague awareness of black music – attempting in patches to be "funky", pre-empting Bowie's infinitely more convincing *Young Americans* by almost a year. Reed was a big Al Green fan, and took the first track's title from a Green song (Green, in turn, had lifted it from Wilson Pickett's standard "Mustang Sally"). A black music "feel" was becoming increasingly popular among rock stalwarts, and "blue-eyed soul" was in vogue. Steve Katz did a fair if unspectacular job on Reed's album, ditching the heavy-metal axe heroes and getting him radio play, but Reed didn't react well to accusations of "selling out", and soon Katz's reward was to be unceremoniously jettisoned. The singer was also falling out with his manager, Katz's brother Dennis.

In the months leading up to the sessions at New York's Electric Lady, Reed had been working hard (touring) and playing hard. He'd dabbled at writing for Iggy, and he'd been in touch with both John Cale and Nico about working together again, but arguments had started almost before a handshake, and these ideas came to nothing. "Lou just wants to be black," sighed Nico presciently. In another brief burst of reconciliation, he'd also asked Andy Warhol to help him with visuals for his live shows, but Warhol was not the same artist he was, and couldn't or didn't deliver, his hands full with vacuous "celebrity portraits".

When it came to the recording, Reed's eye wasn't on the ball and Katz apparently took charge. "I slept through it," he yawned a couple of years later. "They'd make a suggestion and I'd just say, oh, all right. I'd do vocals in one take, in twenty minutes, and then it was goodbye… It was produced in the slimiest way possible."

Katz has responded, "Lou was not totally there as an artist. He had to be propped up like a baby with things done for and around him. Clearly this was the situation he wanted." In 1977, Reed was to tell Allan Jones in *Melody Maker*, "I just can't write songs you can dance to. I make an effort – and *Sally Can't Dance* was an effort. But I despise it." He admitted a fondness for one track, the atypical "Ennui". When the clouds lifted to allow a cheekier humour, Reed cracked, "This is fantastic – the worse I am, the more it sells. If I wasn't on the

Iggy: Reed had tried to write for him

record at all next time around, it would probably go to number one."

But if Reed and others resent the musical accessibility of *Sally*, its very candid lyrics are dark by anyone's standards, and he certainly wasn't compromising there. Often they're more autobiographical than he'd care to admit. "I sound terrible, but I was singing about the worst shit in the world," he griped. "That wasn't a parody; that shit was what was happening." In truth, he sounds great. World-weary, miserable, bitter and twisted, sure, but in Lou Reed's subterranean world these are essential qualities. Put *Sally Can't Dance* on today, thirty years on, and it sounds more intriguing and perversely foxy than ever. To anyone fascinated by Reed's tumultuous early life story, it provides revelatory insights. It's "funky" in many conflicting and charismatic ways.

RIDE SALLY RIDE

"Isn't it nice, when your heart is made out of ice?" Has a line ever so perfectly captured an artist at a specific moment in time? As tinkling pianos and mournful slides usher us in for what at first feels like another visit to *Berlin*, Lou is resigned, but resilient. In another echo of Ezrin's production techniques, descending chord sequences are underscored and emphasised by staccato stabs. Then warm and lovely backing vocals, not too far off gospel, come in for the "ooooh" which kicks the song up a gear. For all the criticisms, there's a fine feel to this album.

The lyrics are savage but witty, suggesting the always-deadpanning Reed sees at last the funny side of some of the debauchery he's witnessed or initiated. After all, who among us hasn't welcomed fresh-meat guests to the house by quoting his couplet, "Sit yourself down, take off your pants/Don't you know this is a party?"

ANIMAL LANGUAGE

Originally called, in drafts, "Mrs O'Riley's Dog", this again laces the vitriol with grisly humour, even utilising poppy hooks like "bow wow" and "miaow". A guitar-led mid-tempo rocker, Chuck Berry with a superbad attitude, it shows off Reed's oddly effective timbre and phrasing. The horn stabs are energetic and splendid; the band seem to be – whisper it – having fun, and there's a vague echo of Bowie's *Diamond Dogs*. The rock'n'roll animal finds his language to encompass an anecdote that's graphic even by his standards: pets are punished, abused even. Ultimately a "dude's" sweat is "shot up" between a hot dog and a wet cat. Cruel, callous, compelling.

BABY FACE

With hindsight, one can hear a bridge between the *Berlin* sound and the *Coney Island Baby* sound here. It's certainly more J.J. Cale than John Cale, with a bluesy-groove shade of Eric Clapton's "Cocaine". The guitar licks point to *Coney Island Baby*, while the broodiness and repetition of "No no no" (compare to "Lady Day") begs reference to *Berlin*. And Reed's vocals are low, even sexy, as "he" – or possibly "Caroline" again – addresses "Jim". Jim's not easy to live with, what with his predictably unpredictable drug intake. Other interpretations have wondered if this is Reed documenting the fall-out of a homosexual affair of his own, but the characters are surely too close to those of *Berlin* to deny the link. "You can keep it!" shouts the dissatisfied lover, with righteous ire.

N.Y. STARS

An astonishing outpouring of evil rancour, over a rock backdrop that resembles both The Rolling Stones' "Heartbreaker (Doo Doo Doo Doo Doo)" and Bowie's *Aladdin Sane*-era guitar grinds. Reed's voice here is camp, fey, sneering, and drowned in reverb or delay. But is he attacking the old Warhol crowd, the Factory's second-string hangers-on, or is the intended target Reed's own disciples/fans? Reed was growing increasingly frustrated at seeing rows of "faggot junkie" impersonators at the front of his shows, and often abused them from the safety of the stage. Here, he may be going one further, insulting them on a record they're buying. The lines which do the most damage are: "They say 'I'm so empty/No surface no depth/Oh please can't I be you/Your personality's so great'." Although, too, "the faggot mimic machine never had ideas" would do the trick and offend the true believers.

But there's also plenty of evidence to cement the theory that this song is a retroactive assault on his former friends and collaborators in Greenwich Village. "A standard New York night," he reasons, is a "fairly stupid thing". Remorseless, he snaps, "I'm just waiting for them to hurry up and die." Perhaps he's even adopting the persona of Warhol himself when he blankly observes, "It's a game … we're very good at games." If the title track is indeed, as seems most likely, about an unfortunate, chewed up and spat out non-survivor like Nico or Edie Sedgwick, this would work.

KILL YOUR SONS

Could Reed – whose picture currently appeared on posters saying "Wanted dead or alive (what's the difference?) – for transforming a whole generation of young Americans into faggot junkies" – still shock with his subject matter as opposed to his increasingly out-there onstage antics? With this sludgy slice of gloom-rock, which possibly inspired Marilyn Manson's entire career, he could. Written years before, "Kill Your Sons" – a hugely influential song on generations of admirers of the Reed canon – is autobiography any way you look at it. Beginning with explicit confessions of his teenage electroshock therapy (the psychiatrists, by the way, were "two-bit" – his favourite adjective for people he doesn't like, which is just about everybody), which so clearly failed to "cure" his homosexual tendencies, he describes how it immediately

affected his short-term memory. He couldn't even read a book without having to start again once he reached page seventeen.

In the next verse he has a pop at his parents, hinting at violent acts by his father, before, for good measure, dissing his sister and her husband – "he's big and he's fat and he doesn't have a brain". Now there's a line that suggests Reed's inner child is still stroppily kicking and screaming. There's the usual litany of drug references, before Reed justifies this wanton act of regression. The parents, he feels, kill their sons "until they run, run, run, run away". Ah, they fuck you up, your mum and dad … Reed as Manhattan's answer to Philip Larkin, anyone?

Come to think of it …

ENNUI

"'Ennui' is not bad," Reed told Allan Jones in the midst of a tirade about how much he loathed the album as a whole. "I change my opinion of the album with the mention of that song. I like 'Ennui', there's always an isolated moment on every album that I really like. It's the track that most people skip, I suspect. It must be, it's the one I like."

Ennui: a French noun popularised by poet Charles-Pierre Baudelaire. Roughly translated it means a state of mind comprising will-fogging boredom and existential restlessness, from which one craves escape, by any means. Often transgressive sex or drugs. Especially transgressive sex or drugs.

Like "Baby Face", "Ennui" floats on a forlorn mood we've previously encountered on *Berlin* (although the melody actually borrows fragments of "Make Up" from *Transformer*). It has instant gravitas. A mellow bass and slide guitars understate the emotion; Reed's voice is so low it physically rumbles. The choir effect that comes in is thus all the more beautiful.

Again, Lou berates all the kinds of people who

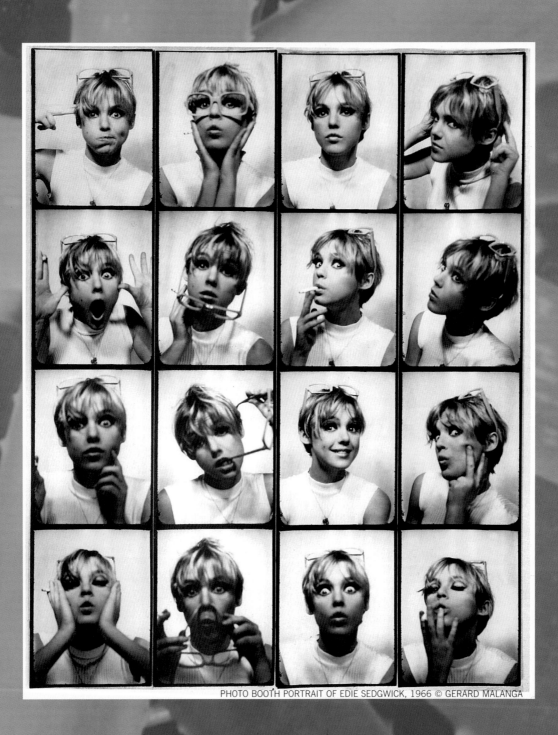

PHOTO BOOTH PORTRAIT OF EDIE SEDGWICK, 1966 © GERARD MALANGA

are ... well, like him, I guess. Promiscuous, desperate, pained. "Pick up the pieces that make up your life," he advises, in conclusion. "Maybe someday you'll have a wife." And then, in one of the most superbly arch (and autobiographical) punch lines in narcissistic rock history, he adds, "And then alimony." It's so unexpected, funny and tragic that you can't believe he's said it in the context of a song. But then Reed's greatness has always been saying things in song that just cannot be said in song. "Ennui" is one of his many accidental, not-trying-too-hard masterpieces. "It's the truth."

SALLY CAN'T DANCE

Characterised by sleazy, stuttering guitars, hot-blooded horn stabs, more lyrics about violence, rape and nasty, doomed, suffering people – this was obviously the one to release as a single. In fairness, it did its job in promoting the album (well, once you'd heard this, you knew you'd heard it). Its efforts to be soul or funk clearly don't cut it, but the gap between its ambition and the reality is interesting enough, and against all odds it's a decent pop record.

Just as Sally couldn't dance, Reed's own onstage attempts at "dancing" was at this time gauche and

Left: the divine Edie Sedgwick

Above: Andy and Edie

erratic, to say the least. And according to some bystanders he was aware and insecure enough to know it, coming off stage and immediately asking them how his new "moves" looked. Something like a deaf Mick Jagger on bad acid seemed to be the general consensus.

Who is "Sally"? A sad St Mark's Place character who takes so much meth she can't get off the floor, who's a trendsetting It Girl but gets raped in Tompkins Square ("real good" – what can one say about those macho misogynistic asides of Reed's except: let's hope he's playing the I-was-acting-a-character defence … and anyway they get worse on subsequent albums), who wears trash jewellery and "balls folk singers"? It could be Nico, it could be any of many Andy Warhol crowd extras.

More likely, it's Edie Sedgwick, whose decline from Andy's ultimate superstar and dancing gamine who dated Bob Dylan to bloated junkie who died forgotten and young is well and distressingly documented in the film *Ciao, Manhattan*. It would be just like Lou Reed to recall a faded former friend coldly, gracelessly and unsentimentally.

But no: nearly three decades later, writing in the sleeve notes of his *NYC Man* collection, Reed revealed the hard reality. "It was about a thing that happened in New York on the Lower East Side. The short version of the story is these guys shot this girl and put her in the trunk of a car and they went out partying. It names all the different clubs that were hot at the time – it's the only time I did something like that, that was dated… the hot clubs, the hot costume designer, the hot this, the hot that. It's just a take on New York nightlife, including the murder.

"And that's why Sally can't dance. They found her in the trunk of a car."

And anyway, who else but Lou Reed would make a half-hearted stab at coming up with a dance album, then go and call it *Sally Can't Dance*? Naturally, most of the fans who purchased it missed the irony by miles and miles.

BILLY

If "Ennui" is atypical of the album, "Billy" is perhaps even more incongruous. Simple acoustic guitars, lilting saxes, and it's practically a folk song, full of genuine rather than sarcastic self-analysis. It traces the parallel (then less so) paths of himself and his childhood buddy Billy. Billy scores touchdowns, becomes an A student while Reed drops out. Billy becomes a doctor, then bravely goes to Vietnam, while Reed doesn't: "I was mentally unfit or so they say…" But when Billy tragically returns from war, he's a ruined casualty, his nerves are shot. "Last time I saw him I couldn't take it any more… it was like talking to a door."

"Now," muses a for-once earnest Reed, "I wonder which of us was the fool." It's a classic songwriting device, the moral twist at the end. But Reed was smart enough to know about the grey areas. Riddled with self-loathing as he was, he surely wasn't announcing that his lifestyle choices were the sensible ones *vis-à-vis* self-preservation?

Or was he? Onstage he'd taken to a little routine wherein, during "Heroin", he mimed shooting up. There was even debate about whether he *was* miming this act. Then he'd turn on his devoted audience, ridiculing them for buying into heroin myths. He was a ball of confusion. A (bizarrely) commercially successful ball of confusion – though he hated what he saw as a situation where people were buying the outrageous persona, not the music.

So Lou, still wondering which one was the fool, himself or his public image, reacted in the only practical way.

He began a serious affair of several years with a transvestite, sanctioned the release of another live album he had no feelings for, and then recorded the most alienating, abrasive and unlistena sure as hell couldn't dance to that one.

LOU REED LIVE

March **(1975)**

VICIOUS ➤ SATELLITE OF LOVE **➤ WALK ON THE WILD SIDE ➤** WAITING FOR THE MAN **➤ OH, JIM ➤** SAD SONG **Recorded at:** Academy of Music, New York

By January 1975 the hyperactive Reed (that Warhol work ethic still pushing him on) was already roughing out songs for *Coney Island Baby*. He was touring manically, his fans secretly hoping they'd be at the show where he finally toppled over the edge into rock'n'roll suicide. He also crafted away at a long-term "electronic" music project.

Possibly too busy to notice, he nodded his assent as RCA pulled a speedy sequel to *Rock'n'Roll Animal* from the tapes of the same shows at the Academy Of Music. It at least proved Reed hadn't been lying when he said the band then had tackled *Berlin* songs as well as old Velvets numbers, and guitarists Hunter and Wagner were loud and proud (even on "Sad Song"). Press ads at the time read: "You haven't lived till you've heard Lou Reed Live".

They cynically claimed that Reed himself called it "Rock'n'Roll Animal Two", and weirdly concluded: "The sound of it could frighten you to death."

Lou had yet another distraction. The divorcée had hooked up with "Rachel", a transvestite who he described as "a street queen". Lester Bangs was less kind to him/her: "long dark hair, bearded, tits … grotesque, abject, like something that might have grovellingly scampered in when Lou opened the door to get milk and papers in the morning." Others thought he/she was beautiful and elegant. Reed found with him/her a kind of happiness, moved him/her into his gold-disc strewn Upper East Side apartment via his stay at the Gramercy Park Hotel (subsidised by RCA), and honed – if that's the word – *Metal Machine Music*.

METAL MACHINE MUSIC

July **(1975)**

➤   ➤   ➤   ➤
➤   ➤   ➤

Safe to say that any "stories behind the song" volume can hereby use the cop-out clause that *Metal Machine Music* doesn't have any songs on it. Produced and played by Reed alone, predominantly on his home studio, it's a double album full of almost sheer noise and ear-splitting feedback. White noise, in fact, with perhaps a dash of very black humour. It's an anti-record, of anti-music. It's a bad joke, a giving of the finger to his fans and his critics. It's a bonfire, with his reputation on the top.

Reviewers ridiculed it, except for Lou acolyte Lester Bangs, who called it "the greatest album of all time". Possibly, just possibly, for effect.

"It was a giant Fuck you," said Reed. "I put *Metal Machine Music* out to clear the air and get rid of all those fxxxing assholes who show up at the gigs and yell for 'Vicious' and 'Walk On The Wild Side'." You mean the people who liked you and bought your records, Lou?

If Reed thought he was proving he was still in

touch with his Velvet Underground roots, he was also displaying to the world that he hadn't quite grasped that what made the Velvets transcendent was their mix of dark and light, of sweet and sour. This was too extreme. Indeed, it's the answer you whip out when people claim there's no such thing as too extreme. Oh yes there is, and it's stupid, childish and pointless. *Billboard*'s review ran: "Recommended cuts: none."

Reed, never one to admit he was anything less than a magnificent genius, genuinely tried to deliver a parallel manifesto, waffling on about the record's "classical" merits, name-dropping LaMonte Young, Beethoven and Mozart. He alienated and provoked everyone he'd set out to, including his record company and manager. Arguably he really did believe in it – to this day he professes so, saying it was years ahead of its time. Arguably he was just taking the piss.

"Just listen to the melody lines," he has said. "The thing is, no matter what else they say about it, they can't miss the fact that it's so precise… I made it for myself. I love it. This is for a certain kind of people. There aren't many… I find it very relaxing. If I or certain friends are uptight, it relaxes us. So it's a good way of clearing a room. It's NOT done as a joke."

Others confirmed that he had been mooting this idea since the '60s. And now he had the equipment to do it. He claimed it was heavy metal. "Nobody's gonna cover it. I can't see the Carpenters doing their version of it."

Perhaps John Cale approved of Reed's turning his back on pop? Um, no. "There's a lot of impressive disinformation on the back of the cover," said Cale. "But it's trap and I'll avoid it if I can. Electronics is boring, anyway. It should be left to the professionals." Miaow!

As for those liner notes, they remain impressive. Amid lines and lines of speed-addled crap, Reed hits in a few salient, if self-promoting, epigrams. "This record is not for parties/dancing/background/romance. This is what I meant by 'real' rock about 'real' things. No one I know has listened to it all the way through, including myself. It is not meant to be. Start any place you like. Most of you won't like this, and I don't blame you at all. It's not meant for you… For that matter, off the record, I love and adore it…"

There's then one of Reed's all-time classic quotes: "I'd harboured the hope that the intelligence that once inhabited novels or films would ingest rock. I was wrong."

After drifting off into amphetamine rants against the media, politicians and, er, amphetamines, Reed concludes, "My week beats your year."

Later, the arrogance subsided and there were apologies, mumbled (and then denied) statements that the record company had promised to release it with a sticker (or something) saying it wasn't a "rock" release or that it featured no lyrics, no singing, no tunes. "It was ill-timed and misrepresented," he offered, hoping that "my new album *Coney Island Baby* can make up for any difficulties and disappointments caused". And then the retractions were retracted. If Reed had planned this to get rid of manager Dennis Katz, it worked. He quit, to be replaced by booking agent Johnny Podell, a high-flying cokehead.

"That album took a couple of weeks," Reed told *Uncut*'s Nick Johnstone in 2000. "I had amps and a tape recorder. I set up a feedback loop and played with the speed of the tape recorder. I took a real beating over it. It was supposed to have a big thing on it saying 'No Lyrics No Songs No Voice', but it didn't. It just said in the tiniest little letters 'An Electronic Composition', so people ordered it under the mistaken impression that it was something else. So they had incredible returns. But the record stores said, 'We'll never buy any new records of yours – ever, ever, ever again. This is a terrible thing.' People were misled – if they wanted an instrumental album then they should have been told.

"People heard it and were like: Argghh! What is this? Are you crazy? RCA said they'd only let me make another record if I swore it'd be nothing like it."

And it wasn't. No one in their right mind will ever listen to *Metal Machine Music* all the way through for fun (although Reed has recently re-recorded it in Germany and, convinced it's not so crazy in 2004, is threatening to put out the new version). It could have made its anti-everything point in much more

intelligent ways. "Sister Ray" already had. But perhaps Reed's best and most rational defence for it came when he said, "It was all so boring – then along came *Metal Machine Music*. It was like a bomb. The idea was good in itself, but for the full impact you had to go through all the motions of execution."

Most of us would have been perfectly happy if he'd settled for the mere idea.

CONEY ISLAND BABY   _{Dec '75 (US)} (1976)
Jan '76 (UK)

CRAZY FEELING ❥ **CHARLEY'S GIRL** ❥ SHE'S MY BEST FRIEND ❥ **KICKS** ❥ A GIFT ❥ **OOOHHH BABY** ❥ NOBODY'S BUSINESS ❥ **CONEY ISLAND BABY** Produced: Godfrey Diamond and Lou Reed
Recorded at: Media Sound Studios, New York **Musicians**: Lou Reed (vocals, guitar); Bob Kulick (guitars); Bruce Yaw (bass); Michael Suchorsky (drums); Godfrey Diamond (various).

There's rarely the kind of correlation you might expect between Reed's life and work. Just when it seemed he'd turned his back on accessibility and bitten the hands that fed him, he grovelled back to RCA with this tender, sweet, more-than-listenable album. Doubtless, Rachel was the muse. Vastly underrated, it's a lovely journey through doo-wop and soul as refracted through Reed's psyche. Amid the gentler grooves, a couple of still-sharp fangs can be glimpsed. And if any lead guitarist wants to know how to play a lot, but subtly, without ever lapsing into tastelessness, Bob Kulick's licks here are textbook. *Coney Island Baby* is, however, generally remembered for the incongruous shocking aggression of "Kicks" and the touching vulnerability of the title track's autobiographical candour.

Enjoying his bizarre domesticity with Rachel, Reed seemingly mellowed a tad. Hard to believe, but he'd not only invited Doug Yule to join his 1975 touring band, thus rehabilitating Yule's reputation, he'd also rehearsed and performed with John Cale

at St Mark's Church. He'd held discussions about collaboration with Warhol, but lost interest, suggesting Warhol was nowhere near the creative force he'd once found so inspiring. Reed's hair was no longer blond, now jet black. He was hit by a brick while on stage in Rome: shows were abandoned due to a "nervous collapse" and riots broke out. But generally – everything's relative – things were calmer. Except on the business side of things. The relationship with Katz was beyond repair, and legal action was bandied back and forth. Reed spoke of misrepresentation and fraud, even blaming his personal paranoia on the lies of his management. For his part Katz ordered injunctions to prevent *Coney Island Baby* being released. "I was served with three different subpoenas with this recording," said Reed. "One before, one during and one after." Apart from Rachel, Lou's new best friend was his not-quite-manager Johnny Podell, who'd established himself via tours of duty with Crosby, Stills, Nash and Young and George Harrison.

Reed's comments on *Coney Island Baby* were as confusing and littered with contradiction as ever. "It's me from top to bottom," he offered, "and if you don't like it – stuff it. It has to be accessible." It is. "If you want to make records for a cult of three, OK, knock yourself out, but don't have any illusions. I think *Metal Machine Music* really demonstrated that." On another occasion, uncharacteristically suggesting he was insecure about ever having matched the Velvets, he drawled, "I would have left it with the Velvets and *Metal Machine Music*. Everybody connected with this album knows that to have me record it, it couldn't be tampered with. No outside disruptive forces, no advice, no looking over my shoulder. It's how I used to feel when the Velvets were together." He then backtracked furiously. "But it's not a nostalgia trip. 'Cos the old Velvets stuff was about ten years ahead, so if I start doing my part now, I should be right in touch with… 1979."

"I didn't sleep through this one," he said, still digging at *Sally Can't Dance*, which, ironically, it has plenty in common with. "I could play this to people and be really proud of it."

Godfrey Diamond was a young engineer working at Media Sound, who spoke multitudes when he said, "I hadn't really been a huge fan. I guess I was too young, but I really loved the banana album and *Transformer*." Taught the songs at the Gramercy Park Hotel, he did a fine job against the odds, managing to rub along just fine with temperamental Lou.

Clearly comfortable with Rachel, and oblivious in that respect to the inevitabley unpredictable reactions of others – "ain't nobody's business but my own" ran one lyric – Reed was writing poetry, which was very influenced by Hubert Selby Jr and his seminal novel *Last Exit To Brooklyn*. "I enjoy being around Rachel, that's all there is to it. Whatever it is I need, Rachel seems to supply it. At the least we're equal."

You can't argue with that, and you can't argue with the luxurious laid-back feel of *Coney Island Baby*, an album where Reed sounds like he's finally learned how to chill out and relax once in a while. With the occasional intriguing relapse, of course. It's optimistic. It hails "the glory of love". Reviews were good. James Walcott in *Village Voice* compared it to Jean Genet, William Burroughs, "Warhol chic meets European ennui", Martin Scorsese and Sam Peckinpah! *Rolling Stone* was equally kind. But one review from Pere Ubu singer Peter Laughner damned it as sounding "exactly like an Eagles record… maudlin, dumb, self-pitying…" As if those were bad things…

The double whammy of a hideous feedback album and a borderline slushy ripple of romance were not what RCA had anticipated from their favoured street-poet faggot junkie, and, in debt, he soon had to find a new label. Which he did, with remarkable ease. The durable *Coney Island Baby* is as close to "easy" as any Reed record gets. It reached No. 41 on the *Billboard* chart, a performance he wasn't to match again until 1989's *New York*. The glory of love was seeing him through…

CRAZY FEELING

"No candy floss on this album," grinned the adverts. "Just pure Lou Reed." Which makes you wonder which sections of *Metal Machine Music* they'd considered "candy floss". If anything, *Coney Island Baby* is Reed's sweetest album, and the likeable opening track sets out its sensurround stall. The musicians understate, but every ubiquitous guitar lick counts. It's the antithesis of white noise. Prior to the vocals coming in, this could almost be George Harrison's "My Sweet Lord". And Reed's voice sounds all the better for acknowledging the existence of such a thing as convention here.

It's clearly a love song to Rachel, emphasising their common ground – "I've had that crazy feeling too… I feel just like ya." And emphasising it again, without the bitchiness of earlier love (or love/hate) songs: "You really are a queen, ah such a queen/And I know 'cause I've made the same scene..."

CHARLEY'S GIRL

Doo-wop harmonies proliferate on this album, and the band just slides along letting it happen. At times it's like a pared-down *Transformer*. Over an almost cheeky, impish pop rhythm, Lou warns of the perils of trusting Charley's girl. She's a stool pigeon, a police informer who'll rat on you. Just when we're enjoying Lou's new-found mellowness, he inserts, "If I ever see Sharon again, I'm gonna punch her face in..." You can take the boy out of his seething repression but you can't take the seething repression out of the boy.

SHE'S MY BEST FRIEND

First drafted as far back as 1968 with the Velvets (you can tell from the giggly stoner lyrics), this gets updated with splashes of gay lingo and a deceptively simple arrangement. It feels great: Diamond never got due credit for his one and only Lou Reed production job. Cymbals and toms tease out an intro (if only "Ocean" had been this subtle) before a happy-making blend of rhythm and lead guitars surges in. They crank up a gear for the splendid crescendo, and the spooky-funny call-and-response backing vocals and closing "la la la"s are surely influenced by Bowie. Reed's in fine, confident voice, building up from contentment to a queeny screech. It all dovetails perfectly. "She," whether that be a character from 1968 or Rachel, "understands me when I'm feeling down ..."

KICKS

"Anything can be sex. Getting off is sex. Getting to an audience is sex. Looking is sex. Your body is a framework with infinite possibilities; it's just a question of tapping into one of them."

A sensational, visceral fusion of words and music

LOU AND RACHEL © GERARD MALANGA, 1975

that doesn't sit kindly with the rest of the album but, in reminding us of Reed's dark side, sets up a glorious contrast. The Velvets live. Arguably Reed wouldn't do anything as graphic and sinister as this again until "Street Hassle", or "The Gun" on *The Blue Mask*. Bustling gossipy party voices burble underneath and across the song: we catch passing phrases like "the morning of the show, right?" or "we're sending your replacement" or "take your clothes off". Unsettling atmosphere established, a deft guitar groove ghosts in, softly but solidly. Lou moves right up to the mic, his breath urgent, and, occasionally adorned by sinister, twisted, whooshing effects, preaches the hypnotic power of violence, glamorising it, poeticising its appeal. He – the narrator – gets it, understands and tries to convey the allure of murder. How it gets "your adrenalin flowing". After a stabbing, "when the blood come a-down his neck/Don't you know it was ah better than sex/It was a way better than getting laid/Cause it's the final thing to do now." It relieves boredom, he adds. Horrifying. But six minutes of the most arresting sounds you'll ever hear.

Coney Island Baby is a lovely album, but a lovely album of Reed doing what doesn't come entirely

naturally to him. "Kicks" is him doing what he does best. It's intense.

A GIFT

At first, fans weren't sure how to take this – superficially a gloat about what a charming ladies' man and seducer our Lou Valentino was. Then we realised: it was a joke, a self-parody. It was OK to chuckle. It was allowed.

"There's a song which goes, 'I'm just a gift to the women of this world'," Reed told an interviewer. "I love that song – it's so funny. One is supposed to improve with age like good wine. I'm sure I do."

One yearns for the day some unwitting white-bread balladeer covers this in all earnestness, considering its author was waking up every morning with Rachel, or, if away on tour, spending hours on the phone to him/her every night. Meanwhile, it's a gorgeous ironic anthem, draped over a flowerbed of guileful guitars.

"If you don't have a sense of humour," said Reed, "you're doomed."

Probably the greatest song of all time.

OOOHHH BABY

A catchy pop fling that again recalls the jauntier moments on *Transformer*. As you can glean from the title, it doesn't bear much zealously rigorous analysis. Just bathe in those fantastic harmonies. To Lou's delight, the Platters and the Inkspots are eating their hearts out. Its tales of topless dancers and massage parlours on Times Square seem almost by-numbers.

NOBODY'S BUSINESS

A lolloping easy lazy blues that eventually finds a spring in its step. A riposte perhaps to those who gawped at his romance with Rachel. "Rachel knows how to do it for me," he said of the person he met one late night in a Greenwich Village club when he was on one of his speeding-for-days-

before. Rachel's something else." Later he told photographer/journalist Mick Rock, Rachel was "completely disinterested in who I was and what I did. Nothing could impress her. He'd hardly hea my music, and didn't like it all that much when he did." Vaguely reassuringly, even Reed seemed uncertain as to which gender pronoun to use.

CONEY ISLAND BABY

The *pièce de résistance*. Soul, doo-wop and glistening guitars (every interjection a jewel) combine to provide the backdrop over which tough-guy Reed drops the veneer and comes clean about his youthful dreams, new-found love and emotional vulnerability. This is the animal's true serenade. Oddly (in retrospect), it briefly became something of a gay liberation anthem in New York, being interpreted solely as a love song to a drag queen.

First, there's a spoken monologue (conversational intimate), then a tender tribute to the Harptones, "Glory Of Love", one of Reed's favourite golden oldies which lit the fuse. This is six and a half minutes of Reed going out on a limb to open up his heart.

Who'd have had "faggot junkie" Reed pinned as having "wanted to play football for the coach" when he "was a young man back in high school"? God is in the details: "They said I was a little too light to play line backer, so I'm playing right end." He wanted to impress this coach. An early – more physical – Delmore Schwartz figure?

Then the redemptive power of love – not to get too Jennifer Rush – is psalmed. It redeems even when those "two-bit friends" (again with the "two-bit") have "ripped you off". It redeems when people are saying, as they had been of Reed, that "you ain't never gonna be no human being". And it redeems even though "the city is a funny place – something like a circus or a sewer", because when push comes to shove, "different people have peculiar tastes". Certainly Reed's own

As the sublime guitars wind down, like curls of smoke, Lou exhales a stunning, guard-dropped dedication: "I'd like to send this one out to Lou and Rachel, and all the kids in PS 192 … Man, I swear I'd give the whole thing up for you." After years of masterfully malevolent (if defensive) sarcasm, cynicism and satire, of being the detached, cold observer, Reed was daring to care and engage, and to let his audience know about it. His emotions were for real. That he'd been relaxed into one of his most inspired and sensitively audacious songs by an affair with a transvestite just added to the sense of the surreal that flavoured everything Reed did in the '70s. Lou and Rachel may have been secretly strapped for cash, but for a moment, somewhere amid the buzzing, rushing chaos, the living was easy.

ROCK AND ROLL HEART

Oct 1976 (US), Nov 1976 (UK) **(1976)**

I BELIEVE IN LOVE ❧ **BANGING ON MY DRUM** ❧ FOLLOW THE LEADER ❧ **YOU WEAR IT SO WELL** ❧ LADIES PAY ❧ **ROCK AND ROLL HEART** ❧ CHOOSER AND THE CHOSEN ONE ❧ **SENSELESSLY CRUEL** ❧ CLAIM TO FAME ❧ **VICIOUS CIRCLE** ❧ A SHELTERED LIFE ❧ **TEMPORARY THING** Produced: Lou Reed **Recorded at:** Record Plant, New York City **Musicians:** Lou Reed (vocals, all guitars, piano on "Senselessly Cruel"); Michael Fonfara (piano, clavinet, organ, arp); Bruce Yaw (bass); Michael Suchorsky (drums); Marty Fogel (sax); Garland Jeffreys (background vocals on "You Wear It So Well"); Oregano Batman (various).

A new label, an impressive live band, a stable relationship, even some bridges being built with old allies – Reed's 1976 could have been a lot worse. Thing is, he was always broke, rarely having more than ten dollars to spend on any given day. He was in hock to RCA for over half a million. "The lawyers were trying to figure out what to do with me".

Just when things were wobbling worryingly, Reed, lucking out, got a call from Clive Davis, head of the burgeoning and then exciting Arista record company. He signed in mid-1976. Lou comically confessed that he'd felt like saying to ex-Columbia Records president Davis, "You mean you want to be seen with me in public?" Lou "knew then that I'd won". Nowadays we probably associate Davis with twenty years of big-lunged MOR pop divas, but at this time he was highly credible. Patti Smith was a fresh name on his roster. The artistic and energetic American version of new wave (slightly pre-empting British punk) was railing against the complacency of bland radio-oriented mainstream rock, and Smith, along with new CBGB's regulars like Television, Talking Heads, Blondie and Richard Hell & the Voidoids, were picking up the Velvets' torch and spitting from the heart with raw, angular guitars and honest, pugnacious yet poetic lyrics. Reed had to be intrigued. Although at first he

sniffed apathetically at this "punk" movement, Davis took him to see Smith (by whom he felt challenged) and Bruce Springsteen (with whom he was, basically, bored). When Patti Smith put out the thrilling, incendiary album *Horses*, Reed cottoned on that he had to charge up his act again. The fact that *Horses* was brilliantly produced by one John Cale probably underlined the notion.

"I'm too literate to be into punk rock," he's reported to have moaned, though he recently vehemently denied all knowledge of this quote to me. "The new bands are cute, but I don't really know anything at all about punk." Nevertheless he became a frequent visitor to CBGB's. More than a visitor, a participant, an *éminence grise*. He watched gigs by the Ramones and Television, was ignored by Tom Verlaine when he offered advice, saw Cale blast through "Waiting For The Man" with Patti Smith at the Bottom Line. He even joined Cale and Talking Heads' front man David Byrne at a show at St Mark's Church, playing "Coney Island Baby" and then – like every other set of musicians in New York at the time – stomping through "Waiting For The Man".

Uncertain how far to go with the flow, Reed began work on his Arista debut, slated to be called *Nomad*. Once again, Warhol was invited to provide cover art, but the idea fell through. Long-term Reed

confident onstage. A bank of 48 black-and-white television sets was used as a backdrop to the band, earning praise for at least an effort to echo the Exploding Plastic Inevitable days. But the show was barred from London, authorities overreacting crazily to other punk "sinners". And before the tour's end, Rachel – serving as Lou's minder/manager – contracted an infected lung, and was then badly beaten, the victim of a mugging. "Rachel's a street kid and very tough beneath it all," commented Reed. Always hostile to journalists, he's said to have been especially insulting during this period – unless they could stay with him drink for drink, in which case he made with the entertainingly egocentric bluster and bravado.

"Lou and I were friends during this period," Clive Davis has said. "I'll never forget he took me on a tour of Manhattan the likes of which I've never had. It was an amazing experience. Seeing Lou Reed's world was a very revealing, eye-opening situation."

"I used to dream in colour," smirked Reed. "A sign of a very high IQ. Every once in a while I'd dream up a fantastic title like *Rock And Roll Heart*." Naturally the album's legacy will always be that ever-so-knowing chorus: "I guess that I'm dumb 'cos I know I ain't smart/But deep down inside I got a rock and roll heart ..."

Interviewed for the 2000 reissue of the album, Reed said, "If you want to know what my life was like then, in 1976, I would say listen to this record: I was super-lithe and virile."

I BELIEVE IN LOVE

"The thing is, my records are for real, but... coming from Lou Reed, 'I believe In Love' is supposed to be a very peculiar statement."

Mildly spoofing his image over a pretty enough melody, Reed advocates good times, parties, music and love. It's jaunty, sure. But we're

and Bowie collaborator Mick Rock was ultimately to do the honours. *Rock And Roll Heart* took under four weeks to write, arrange, record and mix. Reed, defensively, took to championing under-rehearsed spontaneity. It's a spiky, peripatetic album, leaping from fiery rock to swinging neo-jazz. Lyrically, it's slight, relying on a couple of well-judged self-parody jokes.

Reed self-produced, and played all the guitars. It sold OK, was received OK, but was far from the killer statement from The Daddy that Davis had hoped for. That was to come next time. Meanwhile RCA packaged a greatest-hits set called *Walk On The Wild Side*: a decent collection best remembered now for Mick Rock's cover polaroids of Lou and Rachel. Rock also contributed creatively to Reed's subsequent tour, which most witnesses deemed a greater success than the album (thanks in no small part to guest spots by avant-garde jazz trumpeter Don Cherry). The music was increasingly influenced by the bolder end of black music, and Reed was

Mogul Clive Davis with signings Patti Smith and Lou

reminded that this really is him with the wicked gag of "I believe in the iron cross, as everybody knows ..."

BANGING ON MY DRUM

"This kid said to me, he really liked the ideas on 'Banging On My Drum'. And I said, but there are no lyrics. And he said, 'Frustration'. I thought I'd written a song about having lots of fun, fun, fun, but apparently not. *Rolling Stone* said that song was all about masturbation. Which just goes to show."

Yep, more funtime frolics, but the sense lingers that Reed's trying punk energy on for size without really knowing where to go with it. "The single should probably be this one. It's what the Ramones should do. Three chords is three chords ... but there's a finesse to it." That was something he'd known since "Sweet Jane".

FOLLOW THE LEADER

A facile two-chord chant, but busily tackled by the band (which, despite being mostly composed of the same musicians who played on *Coney Island Baby*, sounds vastly different on this album). Reed had written this in 1971, and in fact had also pressed it into service as the basis of a poem, "The Leader".

YOU WEAR IT SO WELL

"Patti Smith came into the studio at my invitation to hear some playback, and she said, 'How can anybody so difficult write such beautiful things?' Or something to that effect."

Along with "Ladies Pay" and "Temporary Thing", this stands out. It echoes "Perfect Day" or "Satellite Of Love", but is looser, mistier. It has emotion, like the last album. It's not just a tumbling-over-itself muso work-out. Whoever it's addressed to – and old college friend Garland Jeffreys' backing vocals are

Reed meets Blondie's Chris and Debbie

angelic – is maturing, developing "grace and style" in place of pain. Feasibly, it's Reed looking in the mirror. A sunshine-streaked avenue of sorrows he could have explored more frequently. It really is special.

LADIES PAY

It wasn't as sonically adventurous as the Velvets, though Reed seemed to think so. "There's a guitar solo on 'Ladies Pay' that's incredible. It's not even a solo, it's a part. My horn player does it live but I did it in the studio. It's almost evil the way it goes past; it's like a sound wave. I mean it's right back to the stuff in the Velvets." A terrific melodrama, which gathers momentum as Reed ad-libs the climactic vocal phrases and the band earn their corn. Strong enough to have featured on a more focused album, it's both melancholy and muscular.

ROCK AND ROLL HEART

Reed said it dumbest when he said, "'Rock And Roll Heart' is very danceable, the kind of thing that if you were sitting in a bar, and either wanted to punch somebody or fuck, you'd probably play on

the jukebox." With a more considered production, its mickey-taking humour could have given him a hit single, playing as it does with his image. And it *is* funny, deliberately. Surely Midwest rednecks in droves would've sung along with his put-downs of ballet, opera and "New Wave French movies". All of which these days, in his guise as intellectual academic veteran, he'd be loath to criticise. Contrived, but wonderfully silly.

"There are fanatics who believe my lyrics word for word. But I still don't know the lyrics to 'Rock And Roll Heart' – I make them up as I go along."

CHOOSER AND THE CHOSEN ONE

"The closest to fulfilling his major ambition – i.e. becoming Andy Warhol – that Lou Reed's ever got," wrote Giovanni Dadomo in *Sounds*. "Don't bother with this record unless you're the kind of person that gets off on watching paint dry," chimed in Nick Kent in *NME*.

The first Reed instrumental since the Velvets' "European Son" (discounting *Metal Machine Music*), Reed on light-funk guitar. Why? Such was his mystique that critics analysed what he meant by no words. Even his nothings were considered statements. As nothings go, this is harmless, if not exactly Ennio Morricone. A puny part of his wanting-to-be-black phase.

SENSELESSLY CRUEL

"There's a good line in that one. 'Now the time has come to lay to waste/The theory that people have of getting an acquired taste.' You either have taste or you don't – you can't acquire it." Actually, it's a clumsy, cluttered line. The lyrics seem to blame a failed first love (early rejection) for everything since. "Jungian", Reed boldly claimed. He played piano himself, because "I was looking for an unpolished sound on that track". Objective achieved.

CLAIM TO FAME

With such a title, a Reed firing on all cylinders could have done so much more. It doesn't go anywhere

Patti hears what Lou's saying

much – "spaced out, spaced dead" – and is clearly one of those "songs" busked quickly on the spot. When you've got "You Wear It So Well", "Ladies Pay" and "Temporary Thing" out of a 27-day writing/recording session, there's bound to be an equal and opposite downside.

VICIOUS CIRCLE

"The tour will be a fully fledged attack, a seething assault, germ warfare," trumpeted Reed. "I like to think of us as the Clearasil on the face of a generation. Jim Morrison would have said that if he was smart, but he's dead." The sing was inspired by a poem sent to Reed by a teenage British fan… which kind of shows how earnestly he was taking the lyric side of things here. Apparently the fan was stunned when his title formed the basis of an actual album track by his hero. He was right to be. It's rubbish. Another lonely, unformed, half-idea that Reed was too lazy to flesh out. Reed listed it as his favourite, along with "Senselessly Cruel" and "Temporary Thing".

A SHELTERED LIFE

A genuine comedy lyric to match the title cut. Over an old Velvets reject from 1966, rewritten, Lou revels in self-parody as the band enjoy some *faux* cocktail-jazz stylings.

He's intent on losing his "hometown ways" as he accepts he's never travelled, never taken "dope", never "really" learned how to dance, and "I haven't ever learned to swing". He's been true to his wife. "Not much of a life." Really very funny, mainly because, for Chrissakes, it's Lou Reed singing this. With a butter-wouldn't-melt expression. One of the cuter, wittier tracks.

TEMPORARY THING

As so often with Reed's career, just when you're giving up on him, he trots out a show stopper. Profoundly sinister, moody and visceral, it's rich

with purposeful repetition, a wilful antipathy to melody, and an evil sultry heat. "When I heard the tape of 'Temporary Thing', I thought, oh no Lou, you're right on the edge," said the man himself. "You know, I really play for keeps. I've got more energy now, and I know just where to put it. My band's good, and there's nothing to be done about it – it's just the nature of the beast."

Possibly a song about kicking a sexual partner out of bed the next morning, possibly a love-hate song to a drug rush, "Temporary Thing" is a thematic partner to "Berlin", "Kicks" and the best and nastiest of the dark side to Reed. "Along," he opined, "with the chorus of 'Rock And Roll Heart', my favourite lyric here is 'Where's the number, where's a dime and where's the phone?' from the last track."

The lyrics may be slack by his standards, but the feel is immense, clammy, dirty. "My favourite drug song," he has said recently. "It was hardcore before there was hardcore." "Temporary Thing" stays with you – in your hair, in your pores, in your lungs, under your fingernails, on the back of your eyelids – for days and night.

STREET HASSLE

February 1976 (US),
April 1978 (UK) **(1978)**

GIMME SOME GOOD TIMES **➤ DIRT ➤** STREET HASSLE **➤ I WANNA BE BLACK ➤** REAL GOOD TIME TOGETHER **➤ SHOOTING STAR ➤** LEAVE ME ALONE **➤ WAIT** Produced: Lou Reed and Richard Robinson **Recorded at:** Record Plant, New York **Musicians:** Lou Reed (vocals, various); Stuart Heinrich (guitar); Marty Fogel (sax); Michael Suchorsky (drums), Genya Ravan (backing vocals), Bruce Springsteen (vocals).

Bitterness and contempt for, and yet a keen-eyed compulsion with, the underground ways of existence are always evident in Reed's work. Rarely more so than on *Street Hassle*, a return to critical favour which – despite being very much its own beast musically – saw its hardy attitude embraced by punk. Nick Johnstone wrote in *Uncut* in 2000 that it was "a brilliant, seedy record, littered with self-parody, obscenity and chaotic rock riffs played ad nauseam". For all the impact of the self-flagellating intro, and the dubious comedy of "I Wanna Be Black", it's the epic title track which dominates and resonates. "A cello-led, mini rock-opera, about a hooker overdosing on drugs while turning a trick," thumbnails Johnstone. Reed envisaged it as a cross between Burroughs, Selby, Chandler, Dostoevsky... and rock'n'roll.

By Reed's standards, 1977 was a restful year. Having released and toured nine albums from 1972–76, even he accepted he needed a breather to regroup before that rock'n'roll heart gave out. He still frequently gigged however, and with his mixed-race band fuelling his belief that he had blossomed from pallid beatnik to wannabe black man, was happily leading the songs into a loud mutation of rock, R&B, disco and jazz. After all, he figured, hadn't he and the Velvets already "invented" punk a decade back? He was beginning to obsess over rhythm guitar sounds and – not very punk at all, this – the technicalities of recording.

"You know that Marvin Gaye song, 'Got To Give It Up'?" he demanded of *Creem* magazine. "When Marvin says, 'Here comes the good part,' it's the truth. That rhythm guitarist, Ed Brown, his throwaways are riffs that people would give their left ball for. I tried to do that kind of guitar on 'I Wanna Be Black' – naturally, I fucked it up." He was also experimenting with "binaural sound", a technique developed by a German engineer, Manfred Schunke, which thrilled Reed with its extra zap. "You've never heard anything like it in your life – it's spectacular." He wanted to release another live album flaunting this device, but Davis and Arista held firm for a studio album. Producers and studios chopped and changed, until Reed decided to use the German tapes as a backdrop over which to create a new record. Bizarrely, the producer he knuckled down with was Richard Robinson, who'd done such an amateurish job on his solo debut, and whose wife Lisa had led a critical backlash against Lou when the Reeds and Robinsons first fell out. In the '70s, when Reed said, "My week beats your year," he wasn't kidding.

"Note for note," bragged Reed after completion, "*Street Hassle* is exactly what it's supposed to be. It's not disposable like most records. The situations are real and human, the way Eugene O'Neill might write a song. I wouldn't change a hair on it." Promoting its release, he said, "The album's a lot of fun – lovely music, very dirty, mainstream snot."

He considered it commercial, too. "I feel right in step with the market. I like my trash to sound better than anybody else's trash. My audience always knows they're going to get a Lou Reed record for better or worse. The direction might change but it's always going to bear my stamp."

Street Hassle certainly bore his stamp. While we don't have space to delve into every track here, we do have to look at the outstanding ("Street Hassle" itself) and the controversial ("I Wanna Be Black"). For a sense of the ferocious, overheated tunelessness that surrounded them, bear in mind that "Gimme Gimme Good Times" began the work with Reed sneering at himself as another of his personalities went through the motions of "Sweet Jane". "Hey, if it ain't the rock and roll animal himself," he yucks. "Fuckin' faggot junkie!" Pain equals good times, ran the theme. The voice was tougher; this was a Coney Island Brute. "Dirt" demonised an old Judas. "Shooting Star" and "Leave Me Alone" brooked no compromise, the vocals intimidatingly intense. "Wait" was a humourless parody of '60s Spector-stimulated girl groups. "Real Good Time Together" was a radical remaining of a feel-good Velvets party piece, "We're Gonna Have A Real Good Time Together", which Patti Smith had co-opted as a crowd pleaser. Reed toyed with it like a cat with a wounded mouse; rarely can an invitation to fun and games have sounded less irresistible.

Reed was again burning up and playing mind games with his public image, screaming with frustration at how limiting his audience's expectations were. *Street Hassle* wasn't commercial at all, but, brilliantly marketed by Davis (who even released the title cut as a twelve-inch single) as the return of the king of punk, won universal acclaim. After this, Reed really did change.

I WANNA BE BLACK

Controversial, Lou Reed? "I wanna be black, have natural rhythm/Shoot twenty feet of jism too and fuck up the Jews," it starts off, over daft disco style rhythms. And later: "I don't wanna be a fucked-up middle-class college student any more/I just want to have a stable of foxy little whores." There's more stuff about penis size, and:

"I wanna be like Martin Luther King, and get myself shot in spring."

"Nobody could possibly take it seriously," stated Reed. "My producer said that no good would come of this, but the ideas… are hysterically funny to me." So enamoured was he of the song that he originally thought of sharing its title with the album. He'd written the song – or a rough draft of it – as early as 1974. He still loved to shock, and any fooling around with racial stereotypes was subversive in his book. He was, he reckoned, winding up the po-faced platitudes of white liberals, the blanket awe being granted to the flawed Black Panther movement, and the proliferation of white musicians straining to mimic black rhythms. Which, given *Sally Can't Dance*, was a bit like the pot calling the kettle… um, well, you know.

But is it funny? Yes, it's funny, especially in its extended live incarnation on *Take No Prisoners*. "The object of the song was to really try and get you going," Lou explains on his *NYC Man* sleeve notes. "That was the goal. Consider the time period. Really trying to stir things up a bit. And we succeeded."

Plus, as even as unlikely a source as Nico had commented, Lou Reed did want to be black. Sometimes. At least for a little while. Generations of white teenagers – known transiently as "wiggers" – followed suit. Also Eminem.

STREET HASSLE

"I was there, Bruce Springsteen was there, Patti Smith was there," Reed recalls, on *NYC Man*, of the *Street Hassle* recording sessions. "Everyone was in a different studio. I knew Steve Van Zandt [Springsteen's guitarist] and we asked him if Bruce would do this monologue. And Bruce said sure, and that was that … but don't use my name. I wish all of Bruce's fans had gone out and bought it, but since we couldn't use his name, they think it's me imitating him." He goes on to a more general overview of the eleven-minute epic. "It's divided

into three movements and has different characters talking… here you have a lot of words. The very end speech the character gives is like a Tennessee Williams monologue." Again, on his latest live album *Animal Serenade* (where the track lasts a mere seven minutes), Reed likens "Street Hassle" to the works of Williams – also Burroughs, Algren, Selby and Chandler. He's proud of it. Rightly so.

It was unlike anything else he'd recorded at this point, save possibly "Berlin". He was still, then, mercurial, ambitious, prone to the grand gesture that could result in triumph or folly. Clive Davis in fact – to Reed's initial ire – suggested he stretch it from a brief sketch to a more filmic marathon. And like "Berlin", "Street Hassle" is a towering triumph of tawdriness.

Springsteen's is a brief cameo – "He's fabulous, he did the part so well I had to bury him in the mix … he's of the street," said Reed of an artist he'd previously badmouthed – and the track is really about its astonishing, haunting arrangement and Reed's macabre, mesmeric narrative. A tape loop of

cellos (originally just two minutes long) circles like a hungry vulture. A full string section comes in (highly effectively) for one part. In the first phase, "Waltzing Matilda", a couple make sordid "love"; money is involved. "Neither one regretted a thing," intones Lou blankly, wearily. Genya Ravan (then a hotly tipped singer) provides the backing vocals which enter at this stage. Reed comes in again for the mid-section, which was the song's original draft, with graphic details. They're shocking, even from him. A young woman OD's and our narrator doesn't give a damn. He just wants to get away from the scene so that the cops can't ask awkward questions. He tells her lover, "You just know that bitch will never fuck again. By the way, that's some really bad shit that you came to our place with… you ought to be more careful around the little girls." All heart.

"Bad luck" stalks his protagonists. In "Slip Away", the third section, there's a nod to Bruce with "tramps like us, we were born to pay". Then Reed's cold cynic breaks cover, cracking into a real and

Above: Springsteen: cameod on Street Hassle

sudden urgent plea from the heart – or so it seems. He sings – yes, sings – like he's in a world of pain and confides that "love has gone away … took the rings off my fingers, and there's nothing left to say". He intimated at the time that this was a genuine message to Rachel, with whom things were not now going so well. "That person really exists … and I do miss him."

If, as poetry, "Street Hassle" appears to be three ideas crammed messily into one, it's nevertheless extremely harrowing, and then touching. Lou and Rachel were on the verge of separating. As some kind of compensation, Reed found that *Street Hassle* – a muddled album saved by its scintillating centrepiece – was to win him gushing praise from all quarters.

Obviously he had to go on and shoot his reborn reputation in the foot with another live album, one he described as "one of the funniest albums made by a human".

TAKE NO PRISONERS

Nov 1978 (US)
March 1979 (UK) **(1978)**

SWEET JANE ❧ **I WANNA BE BLACK** ❧ SATELLITE OF LOVE ❧ **PALE BLUE EYES** ❧ BERLIN ❧ **I'M WAITING FOR MY MAN** ❧ CONEY ISLAND BABY ❧ **STREET HASSLE** ❧ WALK ON THE WILD SIDE ❧ **LEAVE ME ALONE** Produced: Lou Reed **Recorded:** Live at the Bottom Line, New York **Musicians:** Lou Reed (guitar, synthesizer, vocals); Marty Fogel (electric saxophone); Michael Fonfara (electric piano); Stuart Heinrich (guitar, vocals); Ellard "Moose" Boles (bass, vocals); Michael Suchorsky (drums); Angela Howell (backing vocals); Chrissy Faith (backing vocals).

"**I** wanted to make a record that wouldn't give an inch … If I drop dead tomorrow, this is the record that I'd choose for posterity. It's not only the smartest thing I've ever done, it's also as close to Lou Reed as you're going to get, for better or worse."

Ever the *provocateur*, Reed launched *Street Hassle* by playing a week of shows at New York's Bottom Line, a relatively "intimate" venue. He taped the shows, and then at Manfred Schunke's Wilster studios in Germany carved a double album from them. *Take No Prisoners* is one of the landmark rock'n'roll live albums. Due to contractual complexities, Arista had to let RCA release it. "This album contains foul language" shrieked the ads; the cover bore an illustration of a street-corner faggot junkie which was so far beyond parody it was almost all the way back to insouciance. Detonated at the height of punk, the record is, by turns, uproariously comical, insanely offensive,

genuinely angry and smarmily sarcastic. "A necessary jailbreak for his then twisted psyche," I wrote in *Uncut* in 2004.

Reed is Lenny Bruce in a bad, mad mood, letting rip at anyone unfortunate enough to have momentarily caught his attention. He hushes the band and breaks off from songs – which are usually very loose jam versions of some of his nuggets anyway – to rant and monologue, generally berating the state of the world, often attacking more specific targets, like members of the audience. In New York society you knew you'd arrived if you were slagged off here. Most rock critics were abused, several by name. Andy Warhol, Norman Mailer and Patti Smith get savaged, apparently just for existing. "Fuck Radio Ethiopia, I'm Radio Brooklyn." Joe Dallesandro gets it in the neck for not being "intelligent" enough. Drugs are getting too expensive. Reed was now living in the West Village on Christopher Street, the heart of the gay community, and obsessing over his beloved "binaural sound", his two dachshunds (a pet-owning affectation he'd copied from Warhol), and his three-year relationship with Rachel, which was irrevocably on the way out. But he seemed most happy when a friend described *Take No Prisoners*

as "manly". Any way you take it, it's one of the most incendiary, bold statements in a career of incendiary, bold statements. It's both a total car-crash and a chewed-up church to the attitudes and contradictions that made the Lou Reed of the '70s unique. He was to make one more album in that decade, before growing up.

THE BELLS

April 1979 (US)
October 1979 (UK) **(1979)**

STUPID MAN ➤ **DISCO MYSTIC** ➤ I WANT TO BOOGIE WITH YOU ➤ **WITH YOU** ➤ LOOKING FOR LOVE ➤ **CITY LIGHTS** ➤ ALL THROUGH THE NIGHT ➤ **FAMILIES** ➤ THE BELLS **Produced:** Lou Reed **Recorded at:** Delta Studios, Wilster, Germany **Musicians:** Lou Reed (vocals, guitars, guitar synthesizers, synthesizer on "Families", bass, backing vocals); Michael Fonfara (keyboards, piano, synthesizers, backing vocals, executive producer); Michael Suchorsky (percussion); Ellard Boles (bass, bass synthesizer, guitar, backing vocals); Don Cherry (trumpet, African hunting guitar); Marty Fogel (soprano and tenor sax, ocarina, Fender Rhodes).

"If you can't play rock and you can't play jazz," Reed told the press, "you put the two together and you've really got something." In a career that for its first half is riddled with irrational, impulsive (and wonderfully exciting) *non sequiturs*, leaping between different aspects of Reed's personality, *The Bells* is even more incongruous than most. Now in his late thirties, he divided 1979 between proudly proclaiming his gay tendencies to the media and meeting and courting Sylvia Morales. Hailed as a reinvigorated punk, he moved his music towards abstract musical exploration. Determinedly ploughing his own furrow and comparing himself to Shakespeare and Dostoevsky, he lazily borrowed three tunes from Nils Lofgren and just penned lyrics to those. Big in Europe, he settled as a cult figure Stateside. As always, contradictions flew off his every synapse.

The Bells is commonly dismissed as one of his least interesting albums, an esoteric lull between highs. But you should concur with Nick Johnstone,

who wrote in *Uncut* in 2000 that it's "an album I've always played to death, even though it's one that many Lou fans can't stand".

Reed was still stuck on "binaural sound" – "I would highly recommend headphones for maximum effect," he said – and took off to Manfred Schunke's studios outside Hamburg with his now regular band, the Everyman Band. Noted jazz trumpeter Don Cherry had guested at a few live shows, and was invited to join the sessions. He's a major player in what you hear on Reed's jazziest album, often echoing his much earlier work with Ornette Coleman, one of the youthful Reed's heroes. Timothy and Karin Greenfield-Saunders' sleeve notes to the 1999 CD reissue of *The Bells* fascinatingly inform us that Cherry's first words to Reed were, "We all come from the pussy." Democracy in action.

Like David Bowie's Berlin-based albums of the period – *Low*, *Heroes*, *Lodger* – *The Bells* is Reed's journey into the guts of sound, an authentic attempt

to bend the framework and remould the vocabulary. It also saw the return to Reed's world of Bob Ezrin, producer of *Berlin*, who introduced Nils Lofgren to Reed and supported their collaborations. Lofgren, an acclaimed singer/guitarist, had played with Neil Young and enjoyed some solo success, which was now fading. Years later he was to bounce back as an important member of Bruce Springsteen's E Street Band. "City Lights", "Stupid Man" and "With You" were built on his melodies. "He'd send me tapes, I'd write the lyrics," said Reed, "It worked out very well." He co-wrote the rest of the album with various band members (the first time he'd gladly co-written since Velvets days), except for his very own "Looking For Love", which, curiously, sounds more like Springsteen than Reed.

"City Lights" criticises America's unsympathetic treatment and expulsion of Charlie Chaplin; "Disco Mystic" consists of just three words: "disco, disco mystic". "With You" contains the storming line: "With you, everyone's a sucker/With you, it's fuckee or fucker," and when Reed adopts a weird Cockney accent, suggests a sideswipe at Bowie. All these are entertaining and full of ideas, if bitty and fragmentary. It's the climax of the album that really burns, however.

"All Through The Night" uses the background jangle and drone of party conversation again, as with "Kicks". The buzz is unsettling, disturbing, but Reed then sings with energy and aplomb. It's one of his greatest lyrics, cataloguing the frustrations and impatience of his old friend/foe ennui. It's a glimpse into the mindset of a manic depressive. The phase where Reed blurts, "When the words are done and the poetry comes and the novel's written and the book is done you said oh lord lover baby give it to me all through the night ..." is a real rush. And there's a typical Reed twist in the closing lines: "Why can't anybody shed just one tear for things that don't happen all through the night." It's the "don't" that highlights Reed's cleverness and

distinguishes him from run-of-the-mill rock wordsmiths.

"Families", too, is terrific. Like "Kill Your Sons" it's an exposé of dysfunctional family life, clearly autobiographical, at least to a large degree. The narrator visits his folks in suburbia, only to conclude sensibly that "I don't think I'll come home much again". A mournful refrain mocks the situation, repeating the inane question, "How's the family?"

And then, in closing, there's the nine-minute title track itself, a determinedly extended electronic drone, punctuated with Cherry's wailing tributes to Coleman. Whispers, mumbles, chants, prayers. And ultimately Reed's chipped voice breaks through, reciting an allegedly spontaneous tale of a Broadway actor falling to his death, happily, from a rooftop.

This was Reed's favourite track: they'd brought a twelve-foot-high bell into the studio, and only bassist Ellard Boles was big enough to bang it with sufficient muscle. Reed was also inspired by Edgar Allan Poe's poem of the same name. (More than two decades later Poe was to light the fuse for Reed's baffling concept album *The Raven*.) "*The Bells* is about a suicide, but not a bad suicide," remarked Reed. "It's an ecstatic movement. It's a guy who's in love with Broadway, and he's on the edge of a building, and he looks out and thinks that he sees a brook, and says, 'There are the bells' ... and as he points, he tumbles over a drum roll – it's beautiful."

"I love that lyric," he recalled to *Uncut* magazine. "It was ad-libbed on the spot, in one take, which was fun to do. It's interesting to just come up with it, whatever it is, wherever it comes from." On his *NYC Man* notes, he states, "It was supposed to be a little rock mini-symphony. The whole thing is a mood piece that's supposed to cause an emotion, and then when I get to the vocal, that was extemporaneous, which has always amazed me. A lot of times in the studio I'll make lyrics up on the spot, and it's one shot, one shot only. No second take because I can't do it a second time."

The Bells, not an easy listen, has true *noir* atmosphere, and is worth peering into. It's a kind of detour onto The Road Not Taken for Reed. From now on, as the '80s beckoned, he was to stick to the straightforward song format. "*The Bells*," reckoned Lester Bangs, "is the only true jazz-rock fusion anybody's come up with since Miles Davis's *On The Corner* period." Mind you, Bangs was also to write in his review of the album, "Reed is a prick and a jerk-off who regularly commits the ultimate sin of treating his audience with contempt." Read further, though, and he adds, "He's also a person with a deep compassion for a great many other people about whom almost nobody else gives a shit... there's always been more to this than drugs and fashionable kinks, and... suffering, loneliness and psychic/spiritual exile are great levellers."

Life went on for Lou Reed: after refusing to go on with a show in Berlin until a member of the audience he had taken a dislike to was ejected, he found himself staring a full-blown riot in the eye. He was arrested, charged with incitement, and thrown into the back of a police van. After a London show he got into a hissy tiff with David Bowie, thumping him about the head. The incident was observed by Allan Jones of the *Melody Maker*, who reported it in one of the all-time great funny-though-it-really-shouldn't-be rock anecdotes. "Lou Bops Bowie! Shocking Scenes In Chelsea Restaurant", blazed the "music bible"'s front page.

More peaceably, and surprisingly, Reed bought a small farm in the New Jersey countryside, took to gazing at the stars at night (the ones in the sky), and developed an enthusiasm for the aesthetics and discipline of t'ai chi and Chinese boxing. Soon – and this is where it gets really strange – he was into health food, good long walks, and getting to know artist/designer Sylvia Morales. He'd met her at an S&M club, but their romance wasn't so much "Venus In Furs" as "Sunday Morning". On Valentine's Day 1980, they married. The bells, implausibly enough, were ringing for Reed and his gal.

Nils Lofgren: contributed to The Bells album

GROWING UP IN PUBLIC

April 1980 (US)
May 1980 (UK)   **(1980)**

HOW DO YOU SPEAK TO AN ANGEL ➤ MY OLD MAN ➤ **KEEP AWAY**➤ GROWING UP IN PUBLIC ➤ **STANDING ON CEREMONY** ➤ SO ALONE ➤ **LOVE IS HERE TO STAY** ➤ THE POWER OF POSITIVE DRINKING ➤ **SMILES** ➤ THINK IT OVER ➤ **TEACH THE GIFTED CHILDREN** Produced: Lou Reed and Michael Fonfara **Recorded at:** Air Studios, Montserrat **Musicians:** Lou Reed (vocals, guitars, background vocals); Michael Fonfara (keyboards, guitars); Ellard Boles (bass, background vocals); Stuart Heinrich (guitars, background vocals); Chuck Hammer (guitars); Michael Suchorsky (drums).

Sylvia, as his wife and manager, was to radically alter the direction and tone of Reed's music and writing. He had one last confessional, drink-driven album left in him before getting hitched and hitting the Alcoholics Anonymous meetings. It's an album where he takes a long, hard, but often humorous look at himself and his various personalities before turning forty and, for my money, losing the fire.

"I wouldn't want to be younger. I know more things. When I was eighteen I was really just walking into walls all the time," he said. And then, less plausibly, "I'm a great one for commitment."

Growing Up In Public was a watershed album, and a very witty, intelligent and poignant one, rich with perhaps overcooked (mostly by Fonfara) musical finesse (it's by no means one of his own favourites). Recorded in an alcoholic fog, it's contrarily precise and intricately arranged, often lurching into slick AOR or ersatz stage-musical jiggery-pokery.

It is, as its wry title suggests, where Reed comes to terms with himself. He was to go on to make some fine records, and some dull, even soporific, mature ones. This is the last example of his erratic, neurotic, infuriating and inspirational genius in full bloom. (He's described the opening lines alone as "Burroughs meets Ginsberg in Selby-land".) His oeuvre after this is akin to that of a once-brilliant novelist who misplaces his spark after cleaning up his decadent bohemian nature and taking a residency as a creative-writing lecturer at a university. He still has more to say than most people. But not as much as prime Lou Reed.

But before the decline, the album described by Mikal Gilmore in *Rolling Stone* as, "summoning the courage to love, and along with it the will to forgive everybody who ever cut short your chances in the first place. Reed's entire career – more accurately his entire life – has been leading up to [this]. It may or may not be his finest album, but it's surely his hardest-fought victory." Reed – a bisexual preparing for his second marriage – wrestles with demons here, but does so with dignified elegance (and eloquence), and surfaces beaming, despite the motif of "never ever let them see you smile". He also cracks some fine jokes about sex and booze.

"There are seven million stories in the city," said the ads. "*Growing Up In Public* is all of them." It seemed the record company had wanted to use a slogan left over from *Street Hassle*, for *Growing Up In Public* was one story – the Lou Reed story. Sure, there was the usual fusing of fact and fiction, but the intricate lyrics were hugely self-referential. Of course, Reed blew smokescreens: "I'm so damned sane. Maybe these aren't my devils at all that people are finding on these records, maybe they're other people's. When I start writing about my own, then it could prove really interesting."

Lou with Sylvia

"The songs," he also claimed, "are a composite picture of a certain kind of personality, not necessarily mine." He praised George Martin's Montserrat studios, "right in the middle of nowhere", but notions of fresh air and professionalism were challenged by the nonstop drinking of Reed and buddy Fonfara: "We both almost drowned." Years later, sobered up, Reed recalled that this band, who served him well for years through a bewildering array of musical styles, were more into jazz and funk than rock, and as a guitarist he didn't gel with them. It'd been an interesting exploration for him, this album, but the last verse in a chapter. It was also his last album for Arista before returning to RCA.

If Sylvia's influence was from here on to make Reed more selective about what he revealed, to stop him touring and being tempted by drink and drugs, to edit his creative instincts and encourage him to start writing about big important topics like Society and Politics and Issues and Mortality, *Growing Up In Public* is to be treasured (despite the music's occasional dynamic forays into Kids From Fame grandstanding) as one of the last pages we saw from his private diary, from his personal notebook full of poems, from his inner wild child.

Putting him on a Caribbean island with his Everyman Band sidekicks, where the studio was open round the clock and waiters served the musicians cocktails for breakfast was a bold move by Clive Davis. Reed and his team responded by drinking Montserrat dry, almost as if they knew it was a last glorious fling of sorts. The power of their positive drinking led to some of Reed's greatest lyrics springing forth. *Growing Up In Public* is both a clever, Wildean concept album and the artist's stag night.

HOW DO YOU SPEAK TO AN ANGEL

The tone is set for the album's production and arrangements: all glistening pomp-rock, piano pirouettes and dovetailed dynamics. Prissy fills and tricks (from a cappella sections to handclaps) everywhere, multiple backing voices, dynamics on overdrive, the *de rigueur* band rock-out gorge as a crescendo. It's nearly … Queen! But go with the album and you're rewarded. Even Lou's misguided attempts to belt it out like a "proper" singer bear a certain cock-eyed charm.

A boy is cursed by being born to a witchlike mother and a "weak, simpering" father, thus rendering him shy for life. So how is he expected, Lou asks, to know how to woo pretty girls? "How do you dance on the head of a pin/When you're on the outside looking in?" It's a dazzling piece, both pretentious and purposefully real.

MY OLD MAN

Reed was later to cite this, along with the title track, as his favourite lyric. The music's overblown, but the song savagely criticises his (we assume) father. The boy wanted to be like him, but watching him bully his mother, can't stand it any more. At last the boy ridicules him for having the gall to tell him, "Lou, act like a man."

Like *Coney Island Baby* or parts of *The Bells*, the mix of nostalgia and regret is blisteringly bittersweet. As autobiography, many of the album's songs would contradict each other, so we have to believe their author with his denials. But he's smart enough to know the use of his first name in that payoff line gives it intensity and impact …

KEEP AWAY

Who else would dare to rhyme "a puzzle by Escher" with "Shakespeare's *Measure For Measure*"? Jealousy and possessiveness are dissected here. At first he's solemnly swearing that he'll keep away from good times and fun and old-time friends (the missus waiting on the stairs with the rolling pin?) before twisting the conceit brilliantly to declare that, however, if he's forced to "keep away from everything that's good", he'll "not see you any more" and turn the tables by keeping away from the person addressed.

The irony is that in subsequent years Reed, perhaps unwittingly, fulfilled his own prophecy: "I'll keep away from abstracts, I'll keep it all inside/Well I'll just wrap me up in butter and melt me on a shelf/I'll fry in my own juices I'll become somebody else."

GROWING UP IN PUBLIC

"… with your pants down". True, Reed had endured a nocturnal life in the harsh unforgiving light of the public eye. But he'd revelled in it, much as he lashed out. The song's as comical as it is caustic. Much of it reads like prose, castigating "quasi-effeminate characters in love with oral gratification" who "edify your integrity so they can play on your fears". Again, a disowning of earlier mentors, from Warhol to Bowie. Lou questions what makes a man a man, wondering if the whole concept of manliness is a joke. He's left "caught in the middle", comparing himself to the ultimate procrastinator, Prince Hamlet. He has decisions to make.

It's Lou's wordiest album, and the one where – despite a couple of howling contrivances – he comes closest to being the great American novelist he sometimes sees himself as. Not until *New York* was he to get so overtly literary again.

STANDING ON CEREMONY

A vinegar-soaked vignette about how family members can be too polite and repressed to openly communicate with each other, even in times of physical and existential crisis.

SO ALONE

Both distressing and very funny, this is Reed's most overt dig at feminism and its perceived double standards. It also lampoons the narrator, a self-serving seducer, pretending to be sensitive so as to get laid. At first he's all ears, a shoulder to lean on while she complains about her lover. As she becomes increasingly vocal in her man-hating, his patience snaps. "You said you were very vexed, and you told me to forget about sex/You said you liked me for my mind, well, I really love your behind." He takes her dancing, and when even he is weary of "animals staring at your cleavage", suggests they simply sleep chastely together. "Who wants to be alone?" It's a short story, or an early David Mamet play rejigged by Woody Allen.

LOVE IS HERE TO STAY

A more optimistic romance, but tinged with comic realism. The boy and girl have different tastes, but love will win the day. "She likes Truman Capote, he likes Gore Vidal…" It's a bit of a giveaway, for those seeking autobiographical references, or even fans of *The Raven* (whoever you are), that "he" likes Edgar Allan Poe…

THE POWER OF POSITIVE DRINKING

A wilfully silly song, but a worldly, wisecracking anthem to the joys of booze. The title – playing on the noted self-help manual *The Power Of Positive Thinking* – had been used before in Mickey Gilley's 1978 country hit, but only Reed could have conjured up "candy is dandy but liquor makes quipsters" and the inappropriately dry, "People say I have the kind of face you can trust." If "liquor kills the cells in your head", he concludes heroically, "for that matter, so does getting out of bed". A ballad for barflies everywhere.

SMILES

In which Lou explains why he rarely – never? – smiles. It was drummed into him as a child, by his mother, apparently. It may work for quizmasters or politicians, but he's conditioned to think of it as a sign of weakness, for which "they'll always put you down". Explains a lot, huh?

THINK IT OVER

A remarkable, fragrant, sincere love song, in which it seems Reed documents his proposal to Sylvia. Over a cutely paced and poised tune, he praises her beauty, and wakes her in bed to spontaneously suggest the splice. She, while pleased, recommends realism – that while they've come far, they're not yet in an ideal world, and they must both think these things through before taking a leap of faith. The conceit works beautifully, and Reed sings with a deftness of touch few can have imagined him capable of as recently as... well, as recently as earlier on the album. A little polished jewel.

TEACH THE GIFTED CHILDREN

An *homage* to Al Green's "Take Me To The River", the music rippling in and out of that piece (also famously reworked by Talking Heads), and even its lyrical refrain. Reed adored Green, but here subverted any feel-good themes with a reminder that children should be taught not just about "sunsets" and "moonrise", but also about "vices" and "wages of sin". And, optimistically, "forgiveness" and "mercy". In lesser hands this might have lapsed into platitude, but Reed succeeds in both honouring the great Al and putting his own personality into play again.

This was an album which, without ignoring harsh truths, found Reed engaging in not just much powerful drinking but also some positive thinking. His marriage's honeymoon period yielded strong, sinewy writing of real substance. If anything, Fonfara's flamboyantly incongruous musical settings ushered the words to work harder, and Reed rose to the challenge, though this was the Everyman Band's farewell. Reed was now a different kind of writer, a different kind of musician. All grown up and about to embark on a new phase in his life and career, it was two years until the next release. Whether this made for better music in the '80s is highly debatable.

Actually, it's not. In the '80s, after a promising start, his output was poor, was diluted.

THE BLUE MASK

February 1982 (US)
June 1982 (UK) **(1982)**

MY HOUSE ❧ **WOMEN** ❧ UNDERNEATH THE BOTTLE ❧ **THE GUN** ❧ THE BLUE MASK ❧ **AVERAGE GUY** ❧ THE HEROINE ❧ **WAVES OF FEAR** ❧ THE DAY JOHN KENNEDY DIED ❧ **HEAVENLY ARMS** Produced: Lou Reed and Sean Fullan **Recorded at:** RCA Studios, New York **Musicians:** Lou Reed (vocals, guitar); Robert Quine (guitar); Fernando Saunders (bass); Doane Perry (drums).

"This business of 'dark' ..." muses Reed on his *NYC Man* notes, referring to *The Blue Mask* but also to his work in general. "Life is made up of a lot of things. You could write about moon and spoon forever, and leave any other realistic feeling you have out of the songbook. I don't understand why you would, and yet if you include the rest of your life in it you're called negative, dark.

"It's amazing to me ... for example, I don't know anyone who has a pulse who hasn't experienced being anxious. I mean, unless there's someone locked up somewhere, happy all the time. There's a Yin and a Yang to things, ups and downs. I wouldn't call them dark. I'd call them real life."

The Blue Mask is an album of contrasts – of violence and peace, of trepidation and trust. A heaven and hell for guitar buffs, it's Leonard Cohen fronting Television, it's John Lennon helming Crazy Horse.

Married, going fishing, exercising and eating well, Reed was a new man. He began to tone down the candid, soul-searing narcissism of his writing, and to hone his music, keeping it focused, straight, accessible. While there were still a few errant guitar hailstorms oozing out here and there, he was a more centred artist from the dawn of the '80s onwards. He began to look outward at the world around him as much as at himself and his troubled past. Forsaking drinking, drugs ("the most terrible thing") and touring, he believed in his future, lightened up. Doubtless this has been good for him, and he's lived to a greater age in better health than anyone would've predicted during the *Rock'n'Roll Animal* era. Many critics think his music has got better and better, at least from *New York* onwards. I don't. I think the minute he grew up was the minute his music stopped being glorious. It became safely, sombrely good. Just good. No longer an apocalyptic battle between euphoria and angst. Just… OK. He's written some classy lyrics – *New York* again being the best example – but the music, generic mature repetitive rock rituals, has pretty much died.

On *The Blue Mask* he's still there… just. Many believe it's a classic. When it's good, it's lovely. But when it's bad, it's awful.

"There was a big time span between *Growing Up In Public* and *The Blue Mask*," he remembered, speaking to *Uncut* in 2000. "A lot of changes took place. I had a completely new band, a new batch of people, and some time to think about where you go from here." Tellingly, what matters to him is the sound of it, the recording techniques. Not the statements, soul or attitudes. The artist turns craftsman. "It sounds great. I'd started really wanting to do that better. We got a good sound out of that studio, which was the size of a football field. We played really, really loud there. When you were

playing, you could barely hear another person." And judging by the vocals on the title track, he could barely hear himself.

Among Reed's other credibility-killers during his sabbatical, he'd cameoed as a rock manager in Paul Simon's movie *One Trick Pony* (he didn't enjoy it), and written a bunch of lyrics for heavy-metal hucksters Kiss (he mentioned how nice the money was).

Soon Lou had been introduced by Sylvia to Robert Quine, one-time guitarist with Richard Hell & the Voidoids of *Blank Generation* fame. Reed could take him or leave him until he heard him play guitar, and then a strong bond formed. Quine helped shape the new four-piece band, and with Reed back with RCA, they recorded – mostly live, with only vocal overdubs – *The Blue Mask*, to fawning critical acclaim. It seemed that for the peripatetic Reed to have taken two years out had given him the greater kudos and mystique he'd always coveted. Not for the first or last time, he himself hailed it as his best, while *Rolling Stone*'s Tom Carson, under the headline "Lou Uncorks A Great One", gave it that magazine's now-traditional rave. Perhaps they still felt guilty for the debacle of the response to *Berlin*. "The intuitive responsiveness between Reed and Quine is a quiet summit of guitarists' interplay. The notes and noise soar and dive, scudding almost formlessly until they're suddenly caught up in the focus of the rhythm…" That's hard to comprehend. So's the next part: "With *The Blue Mask*, Lou Reed has done what even John Lennon couldn't – he's put his *Plastic Ono Band* and his *Double Fantasy* on the same record. And made us feel that, at long last, these two paths in him are joined."

Yes, but only two. Previously there had been so many avenues.

Not content with her role as manager and namechecks in toe-curlingly embarrassing love songs, Sylvia was suddenly also the sleeve designer. She took Mick Rock's *Transformer* cover and washed it in blue. Her contribution was hailed as "clever" and "witty". You ask me, she just lazily took Mick Rock's *Transformer* cover and washed it in blue. In her defence, RCA screwed up the printing and blew any ambiguities she was shooting for. "I'm very very image conscious and I've tried to use it gracefully, to focus it," Reed is reported as saying in Peter Doggett's definitive *Growing Up In Public*. "On this album I'm bringing all those Lou Reeds together, into one. But the basic image is – and always has been – Lou Reed comes from New York City and writes rock and roll songs."

In stripping away his more baroque pretensions, however, and to an extent hiding behind his guitar (another form of mask), Reed became less of a myth, more of an Everyman. It's what he wanted, as a wordsmith. But it sacrificed what made his music better than good and more than music. Sylvia probably saved his life, and that probably buttoned down his creativity.

At least on this album there were still some startling aspects of his raging subconscious that wouldn't lie down without a mean, dirty fight. It's probably his last bipolar work of art, several shades of moody blue.

MY HOUSE
Dedicated to Delmore Schwartz (1913–1966), this gives us the blueprint of how the guitars of Reed and Quine are going to interact throughout most of the album. Much influenced by Tom Verlaine's Television, though never – as some critics have claimed – hitting the heights of *Marquee Moon*, they're inventive in their ebb and flow. Reed sweetly – almost tweely – describes the beauty of his domestic life, his house, his wife (by name). Then the happy couple contact the spirit of Delmore (true, claimed Reed), who Reed calls, referring to James Joyce, the Bloom to his Daedalus. Over a simple refrain of "our house is very beautiful at night", the guitars do their thing.

But I can't be the only listener who finds the line

"Sylvia and I got out our Ouija board" unintentionally giggle-inducing. And he just about gets away with the saccharine: "I've really got a lucky life/My writing, my motorcycle and my wife." It'd be one thing if he was protesting too much about this state of bliss, but he's not. He means it, and we fear our animal is lost. Thank God he doesn't throw in a couplet about their new washing machine and three-piece suite. And we're supposed to be interested because…?

I mean, everything in its place and whatever gets you through, fine… but this is Lou Reed. Lou Reed. Isn't it?

WOMEN
A kind of follow-up to *Coney Island Baby*'s "A Gift", but not as funny, because trying harder. "I love women, I think they're great/They're a solace to a world in a terrible state."

And thus Reed repositions himself as an all-American regular Joe. Whereas "A Gift" was laden with irony, this probably isn't. He even suggests he might hire a "celestial choir of castratis" (grammatically, it should be "castrati"), to "sing a little Bach". Much earthier is his confession that he used to ogle magazine pin-ups as a kid – "I know that it was sexist, but I was in my teens." This one really does protest too much.

UNDERNEATH THE BOTTLE
An anti-drinking song, presumably ripped from the pages of his own beat-the-demon diary as he strove to give up. Your basic three chords, and the sermon that with booze "things go from bad to weird". The theme is more committedly addressed on "Waves Of Fear".

THE GUN
The album's best cut by a mile, a slither of black magic only Reed could conjure up, and a stunning contrast to the tender sweet nothings of "My

House" and others. Reed's narration is grotesquely deadpan (a compliment) as he narrates a chilling vignette of violence, possibly rape. The track captures the adventurism of the Velvets with the theatrical tropes of Reed's solo peaks. "I write for adults," he's said. Got that right.

A gunman, as far as we can glean, breaks in to a house, threatens rape at gunpoint, forces the woman's husband to watch. It's not pleasant. But the combination of sounds and words has a harrowing, understatedly sinister presence. Reed explained, in response to the reactions the track drew, "The songs are little plays with characters. In 'The Gun', the rapist turns and says, 'Watch your wife … I wouldn't want you to miss a second.' And it's like, what? WHAT!? I've found that, without exception, any guy that listens to that song reacts with universal fear. And it's dangerous for me too. Because… if I do a song, and there's a bad character, or a drug character, or something like that – sometimes it's me, and sometimes it's not. But the thing is, as I sing the song, I go through it. I really do go through it. It's really cathartic in a lot of ways. It's acting. Which I like. But if you do those characters long enough – it can get to you. Some of those lyrics are very rough."

And if "The Gun" implied horrors, the title song on this schizophrenic album was explicit.

THE BLUE MASK

Thrashing chords and flailing feedback on a scale not approached since the Velvets struggle to form a backdrop to a terrifying tale of sadomasochism. No furs soften the blows for this Venus as a boy, who yells, "I get a thrill from punishment." If pain equals pleasure, Reed's enjoying his vocals, where he loses any semblance of discipline, shouting and bawling with gruff, disorientating venom. There's a graphic account of this willing victim's torture, with, as a climax, his finger and his "stallion" cut off. "And stuff it in his mouth."

"Dirty's what you are and clean is what you're not," howls Reed, method acting. For all the acclaim it's been given, the track's a mess which wouldn't have added anything to *Street Hassle* or *The Bells*, and Reed's croaking is abysmal. He's sung badly before, but with unique personality. Here it's not working for him. It's one of those tracks where I feel I may be missing the point, but frankly I'm not about to go and get my "stallion" cut off in order to better grasp the levels of meaning.

AVERAGE GUY

The album calms down again after that. And while we relish Reed being a loose cannon, this time we're content to step back from the abyss. It's the tongue-in-cheek comedian of *Transformer* singing with a slight swagger here, with a touch of the Kinks' Ray Davies, whom Reed had long professed admiration for. Of course the big joke is that it's Reed claiming to be an "average guy… trying to do right… trying to stand on his own two feet" – and the bigger joke, which he's only partially in on, is that outside the shivers of "The Gun" and the title song, *The Blue Mask* album is where he starts to convincingly resemble the Everyman he's gently mocking, worried about his liver and his bowels.

THE HEROINE

A solo demo – just Lou and guitar. The band had recorded a version, but Sylvia preferred this, and her word – it seems – was law. Part love song, part dreadfully gauche wordplay regarding the Velvets' "Heroin" which doesn't come close to working, it's nervous, hesitant, and easily forgotten.

WAVES OF FEAR

A catalogue of the obstacles facing anyone kicking addictions, typically graphic and credible. He's suffocating, sweating, drooling, choking, cringing, looking for his pills. Panicking while Quine's inspired guitar burns.

THE DAY JOHN KENNEDY DIED

A rather cheesy where-were-you-when-JFK-was-shot ditty, recently revived for the *Animal Serenade* album. Not that Reed had ever, like, voted for the golden boy or anything like that. As with so many rock stars, he was given respect for insight merely for mentioning an icon's name. For lip service. And Reed is disingenuous when he claims he can't comprehend how someone could have shot Kennedy: his entire recorded output has already examined these irrational inhuman thrusts. "I dreamed that there was a point to life and the human race," he drawls, over nursery rhyme chords.

HEAVENLY ARMS

"Only a woman can love a man in a world full of hate… Sylvia…" Touching love letter to his spiritual saviour? Or excruciatingly embarrassing slice of mushiness? I confess that on the album's release I couldn't believe Reed had sunk so low, but everyone around me deemed it lovely, so I kept quiet. But short of bursting into a chorus of "Oh Yoko, you're my everything" he could hardly be less … cool. It kind of makes a mockery of many of his earlier songs and stances. The romantic blurts on "Coney Island Baby" and "Perfect Day" worked because they strained against the tide. This is just wet: if she was any kind of woman she'd have nipped it in the bud, or at least kept it behind the Reeds' closed doors.

As Adam Sweeting wrote in *Melody Maker*, "It would be romantic in a seedy sort of way to think that Lou was a doomed genius, twisted in a knot, (still) driven to drink by assorted demons… but really the truth is nowhere near so dramatic. 'Lou Reed Gets Married And Settles Down'… not much of a headline, is it?"

For all the unsettling high spots of *The Blue Mask*, its low spots confirmed that this was the beginning of the end of the Lou we thought we knew. The next album made sure.

LEGENDARY HEARTS

Early 1983 (US)
May 1983 (UK) **(1983)**

LEGENDARY HEARTS ➤ DON'T TALK TO ME ABOUT WORK ➤ **MAKE UP MY MIND** ➤ MARTIAL LAW ➤ **THE LAST SHOT** ➤ TURN OUT THE LIGHT ➤ **POW WOW** ➤ BETRAYED ➤ **BOTTOMING OUT** ➤ HOME OF THE BRAVE ➤ **ROOFTOP GARDEN** **Produced:** Lou Reed **Musicians:** As The Blue Mask, except with Fred Maher on drums.

A listless, sagging affair, which dismayed those who'd proclaimed *The Blue Mask* as the dawning of a brave new Reed world, and compounded the doubts of those who'd embraced it less vigorously.

"I like the idea of 'Legendary Hearts'," Reed was to say of the plodding, country-influenced title song. "It's like looking at Romeo and Juliet in an idealised *West Side Story* version of it, then looking at a New York City East Side version. Which, by the way, was just a hop, skip, and jump from the *Berlin* characters."

Certainly this lacklustre work lacked the intensity of *Berlin*, and similar themes were infinitely better investigated on *New York*. "You've got to fight to make what's right" … hmm. The "A Walk On The Mild Side" headlines and captions began to kick in in magazines everywhere (to this day they're still the default mode for many exhausted editors). "It's very hard to keep things simple," Reed had said, but it seemed fairly straightforward for him here. Another lousy Sylvia sleeve design, the usual creaking chord structures, a vague sense that marital bliss wasn't all it had been cracked up to be. Also a sense that he didn't dare go as far with that theme as he'd naturally liked, in case Sylvia told him off. Even the riskier, edgier lyrics, like "Betrayed", seemed derivative of Hubert Selby. "The Last Shot" was another strong, bitter, alcoholic's cry, from the resigned point of view of a drinker who knows he'll never be able to quit. Speaking to Nick Johnstone years later, Reed said, "A monstrous song. My God. Wouldn't want to listen to that one. But it was great – it's the perfect rock song. I mean, it does it all. It stays with you.

"I wrote it because I believed it. I'd thought so many times… you know, wishing it was your last shot, this one right here. Of course, nothing remotely like that ever happens. It was just this fantasy. It was absurd. You're talking about life and death stuff. I didn't write it to help anybody, no. Not even me. I just write to write. I don't completely understand it."

Extending this on the *NYC Man* notes, he ponders, "If William Burroughs wrote rock songs … I look at it that way. Movies have covered this, novels have covered this – rock, no. *The Man With The Golden Arm*, old movie, no big deal. Put it on a record, 'The Last Shot' – it's a big deal. Why? Because kids take it more seriously, and because I'm not lying. The movie's a lie. I'm not lying. Everybody knows that about me. Mine is as straight as it goes. For better or for worse, there it is, no kidding around. I walk around the city, so if anyone wants to discuss it with me, I'm here, I'm available."

"Rooftop Garden" carried the immortal line: "No sugar with my coffee/How's your tea?" The problem with Reed's new-found musical simplicity was… it was simplistic. *Melody Maker* mauled it as "so worthless… crass… childish", going so far as to call the album "the most insultingly appalling release in years by any major artist". I'm told it might even have been me who wrote that, actually, but I can't be sure. It's not the sort of album where you remember.

LIVE IN ITALY
January **(1984)**

SWEET JANE ➤ **WAITING FOR THE MAN** ➤ MARTIAL LAW ➤ **SATELLITE OF LOVE** ➤ KILL YOUR SONS ➤ **BETRAYED** ➤ SALLY CAN'T DANCE ➤ **WAVES OF FEAR** ➤ AVERAGE GUY ➤ **WHITE LIGHT/WHITE HEAT** ➤ SOME KINDA LOVE ➤ **SISTER RAY** ➤ WALK ON THE WILD SIDE ➤ **HEROIN** ➤ ROCK AND ROLL

Another twenty seconds gone by? Time for another live album, surely. If the UK and US were now brave enough to say so if they thought Reed was marking time, most of Europe still deemed him a god from a higher plane, so any growl or lick was gold dust there. This document of the tours of the time might be enjoyable for zealous devotees of the Reed/Quine band and their duelling guitars, but for most it's a water-treading nonentity. According to *Uncut*'s Reed retrospective in 2000, it "showcased a barbaric slaying of Lou's back catalogue". The mix of Velvets oldies, hollowly sung, and recent Reed material doesn't hang together to any real purpose.

Surprisingly, and emphasising how Reed's priorities differ from those of most fans, both "Heroin" and "Kill Your Sons" made it onto his *NYC Man* collection. Of the former, he notes, "What a great guitar part from Robert Quine… what a great drum part from Fred Maher. I love Fred's drumming." Now there's insight. And of "Heroin", he says, "Two guitars, bass, drums – any band can play this. That's what I like about my songs. You can have the IQ of a turtle and play a Lou Reed song. I love that about rock and roll – anybody can play it, including me. Three chords is good enough; I want to master those. If it was good enough for John Lee Hooker, it's good enough for me.

"But that doesn't mean I don't like Miles Davis or Little Jimmy Scott, or Don Cherry… who I've worked with. So take it with a grain of salt."

Maybe we should have got to the taking-it-with-a-grain-of-salt philosophy earlier. Reed, now splitting up this band (it's usually reported that he was jealous of Quine's guitar technique), was hitting his career's nadir.

NEW SENSATIONS
April **(1984)**

I LOVE YOU SUZANNE ➤ **ENDLESSLY JEALOUS** ➤ MY RED JOYSTICK ➤ **TURN TO ME** ➤ NEW SENSATIONS ➤ **DOIN' THE THINGS THAT WE WANT TO** ➤ WHAT BECOMES A LEGEND MOST ➤ **FLY INTO THE SUN** ➤ MY FRIEND GEORGE ➤ **HIGH IN THE CITY** ➤ DOWN AT THE ARCADE

Produced: Lou Reed and John Jansen

New sensations? Reed was still trying out a few, but with stabilisers on. His hip cache wasn't what it had been, and after the odd buddy acts with Paul Simon and Kiss, he cameoed as a hard-faced self-parody crooning "My Baby Sister" in the *Get Crazy* movie. His throwaway "Hot Hips" featured in *Perfect*, starring John Travolta and Jamie Lee Curtis. This was all a long, long way from his roots, or even from his initial post-Velvets breakout.As if to burn every bridge in one blaze, and desperate for a hit, Reed knocked out the *New*

Sensations album. With Quine gone, he played all guitars himself. The craving for a cheering chart placing was satisfied by "I Love You Suzanne", and "My Red Joystick" followed it up. Some fans find these facile, big-beat, very '80s-sounding pop balloons witty, post-modern and ironic. Others among us think they're unutterably dreadful.

It was the MTV age now, everything Warhol had dreamed of, curdled into a glossy consumerist waking nightmare. Reed, supposed bastion of authenticity, caved in, panting like a puppy dog for "heavy rotation". For "I Love You Suzanne" his video was at least genuinely funny. It began with him in the expected leather-clad punk mode, before, to everyone's astonishment, he mutated into a disco boogie boy, shimmying, twisting and break-dancing through a series of alarmingly agile "moves". That was funny enough, but when Reed swore vehemently that he'd done all the dancing for the footage himself, it became his greatest comic moment since *Take No Prisoners*.

Rubbish album, rollicking comedy. The great record-buying public bought it in herds, and this radio-targeted soulless muzak became his biggest seller since the mid-'70s. Perhaps to a new generation Lou Reed didn't mean what he'd symbolised to the previous one, but to the music industry he was again worth taking a punt on. How he managed to sleep at nights was up to him. For his next trick, he advertised Honda scooters.

"I just wanted to have fun with *New Sensations* …" said Lou. He stressed that he wanted to sell his records, because he really liked them. Irrefutable logic, really. "Plus, if you get into one of my records, there's like seventeen or eighteen others sitting back there. I'm not a bad thing to get addicted to." Means to an end, I guess. Furthermore, when Reed is pressed, he sees himself as a "writer" (though *New Sensations* offered scant evidence of that) – and whether he was "a nice guy, a liar, or immoral" had "nothing to do with it". Sylvia didn't design the sleeve this time. Someone even worse did.

"Turn To Me" was moderately astute, the title cut eulogised his GPZ motorbike, "Doin' The Things That We Want To" acclaimed Sam Shepard's play *Fool For Love* and the films of Martin Scorsese (but, given these fruitful subjects, was a profoundly lame lyric), and "Down At The Arcade" is Reed talking himself up half-heartedly. If 1972's "Ride Into The Sun" said it was hard to live in the city, 1984's "Fly Into The Sun" reckons it's hard to live in "worldly pain". "What Becomes A Legend Most" adopts a contemporary advertising slogan to vaguely comment on the slow decline of a superstar into a paranoid clinging to the vestiges of celebrity.

It's an idea that Lou Reed could have done so much more with. But *New Sensations* is not the stuff of legend.

MISTRIAL April **(1986)**

MISTRIAL ➤ **NO MONEY DOWN** ➤ OUTSIDE ➤ **DON'T HURT A WOMAN** ➤ VIDEO VIOLENCE ➤ **SPIT IT OUT** ➤ THE ORIGINAL WRAPPER ➤ **MAMA'S GOT A LOVER** ➤ I REMEMBER YOU ➤ **TELL IT TO YOUR HEART** Produced: Lou Reed and Fernando Saunders

Even with the archive Velvets outtakes *VU* and *Another VU* reigniting interest in Reed's name, and their influence extending to a freshly dazzled generation of noiseniks, Reed could only manage another turgid turkey. His last for RCA, it underwhelmed public and press alike. Alongside

Reed and back-in-the-fold bassist/guitarist Saunders were J.P. Lewis on drums and Sammy Merendino on programming. "It's very easy to see that the same person who wrote the Velvet Underground stuff wrote *Mistrial*," argued Reed defensively. "It's not all that different; it's just a little older." It was wheezing. It had its bus pass.

Had he achieved anything else in the two years since the inglorious commercial success of *New Sensations*? He'd appeared at Farm Aid in 1985 and supported Artists United Against Apartheid and Amnesty International. He joined such artists as Sting, Peter Gabriel, U2 and Bryan Adams onstage for communal liberal sing-alongs. He'd taken part in New Music Seminar forums, accepted now by the industry as a clean-nosed gent, and eased into the role of elder statesman. He grinned benignly at MTV interviewers, contributed cover versions to mainstream movies… basically, he was turning into a Phil Collins who couldn't sing. He toured with

Robert Quine in the band again, with dull efficiency. He quietly went along with the re-promotion of the Velvets' music, but refused to come too close to the other former members, even filming his sections for a well-produced *South Bank Show* for British television in a separate continent to Cale and co. Most bizarrely of all, perhaps, he teamed up with Sam Moore of the original Sam and Dave to cover that duo's old chestnut "Soul Man". Recorded for the dubious comedy film of that name (starring C. Thomas Howell), it is for the listener to decide whether Reed's singing is intentionally or unintentionally funny. For sure it was funnier than the film (and gave him his first UK hit since "Walk On The Wild Side"). He was everything he hadn't been at the time of that song's conception.

Mistrial throws a few darts at "the state of the world", but it's just the sound of a middle-aged man bitching at the television from his comfy sofa. "Video Violence" is a rant against the images show onscreen and their impact on the impressionable – Lou Reed as Tipper Gore. On the title song he begs the people of New York City to accept that he's a reformed character these days: "When I was thirty my attitude was bad." Yeah, and your records were good. "Don't Hurt A Woman" is an unfocused, noncommittal reference to domestic violence, "Mama's Got A Lover" is a pale imitation of earlier, grittier lyrics, while "Tell It To Your Heart" (recently granted undue prominence on *Animal Serenade*) boasts a cute little twist, passably cynical, at the end of its *Blue Mask*-like floatings. "I don't like the production," mused Reed of the album later. "There were a lot of ugly fights going on."

The standout, though, has to be "The Original Wrapper". A verbose tirade against the wrongs and injustices of whatever quantity of the world Lou's been taking in from MTV, its humour lies in Reed's casting himself as the spark that lit the then-burgeoning, now all-conquering, rap phenomenon. Lou – the big Anti-Apartheid supporter who'd once wanted very much to be black, remember – loved rap, and hey, hadn't he "talked" his lyrics before anyone else? Isn't that what had so engaged the world about "Walk On The Wild Side"?

The way he saw it, he'd invented this rapping lark, so why not give it a go? It was a pity about the not-so-"phat" mullet hugging his head, but Lou thought he was street enough to bark this one out. "It was designed to be the all-time rap lyric," he said. "I read it to my friend Jim Carroll [late author of *The Basketball Diaries*] and he said: 'Oh, you already did that with *Street Hassle*.' And I said: 'Oh, that's true'." It attacked Aids, Louis Farrakhan, Jerry Falwell, more televised violence (ironic considering that on the video for the otherwise negligible "No Money Down" he apparently claws his own face till the skin peels away), sports stars on cocaine and "Yippies, Hippies and upwardly mobile Yuppies".

It was either a bit pathetic (grandad attempting to be down like the kids) or a tongue-in-cheek classic of its kind (there are not many of its kind). Blondie's "Rapture" it wasn't. In fairness, Reed is a dedicated hip-hop fan to this day. "I was born in the United States," he spat on the track, "I grew up hard but I grew up straight." And getting straighter by the day …

Disappointed by the response to his last few albums, Reed went quiet. Nearly three years were to pass before his next, which he wrote, rewrote, and then rewrote again and again. And, mercifully, it was to be a real and valid return to form; a bona fide artistic statement from a man who, by looking at what was around him rather than what was inside him, found something to say.

NEW YORK   February **(1989)**

ROMEO HAD JULIETTE **❯ HALLOWEEN PARADE ❯** DIRTY BLVD. **❯ ENDLESS CYCLE ❯** THERE IS NO TIME **❯ LAST GREAT AMERICAN WHALE ❯** BEGINNING OF A GREAT ADVENTURE **❯ BUSLOAD OF FAITH ❯** SICK OF YOU **❯ HOLD ON ❯** GOOD EVENING, MR. WALDHEIM **❯ XMAS IN FEBRUARY ❯** STRAWMAN **❯ DIME STORE MYSTERY** Produced: Lou Reed and Fred Maher Recorded at: Media Sound Studios, New York Musicians: Lou Reed (vocals, guitars); Mike Rathke (guitars); Fred Maher (drums, bass); Rob Wasserman (upright bass); Maureen Tucker (drums on "Last Great American Whale" and "Dimestore Mystery"); Jeffrey Lesser (background vocals); Dion Di Mucci (background vocals on "Dirty Blvd.").

Few artists have been as synonymous with modern New York as Andy Warhol.

Warhol's last reference to Lou Reed in his notorious, posthumously published diaries was: "I hate Lou

Reed more and more, I really do, because he's not giving us any video work." The diary entry is sad in so many ways: Warhol was intermittently working with pop groups who weren't fit to shine the Velvets' boots of leather. Reed had blanked him at MTV awards ceremonies, and, as the diary further revealed, stung him by not inviting him to his wedding to Sylvia. Reed had wanted to move on, a detoxed married man, but had underestimated Andy's sensitivity.

On 22 February 1987 Warhol died in New York Hospital, after what had been expected to be a "routine" gall bladder operation. The wounds sustained when shot by Valerie Solanas had pained him more and more in recent years, but no one close to him anticipated this. He reportedly was dead for over an hour before any of the hospital staff noticed. Only when Andy didn't turn up at the funeral did some long-time friends and acquaintances accept that this wasn't some elaborate pop-art hoax he'd dreamed up. It seems his death affected Reed deeply; he was stricken with the guilt of the pupil who's neglected his mentor. Plans for a musical offering, in collaboration with John Cale, gestated. "Andy's way of looking at things, I miss – I owe him that. His whole aesthetic. If I look at something new and interesting, I still think, oh, I wonder what Andy'd think about it?" said Reed.

Reed and Cale's plans came more sharply into focus when another tragedy befell the ex-Factory axis. Forgotten chanteuse Nico had lived in Manchester (England) for most of the '80s, befriending various bands of the locality, for a while involved in a relationship with the punk-poet John Cooper Clarke, and playing her gloomy music to polite, bewildered and ever-diminishing audiences. Rumours of drug addiction were rarely far away. In July 1988 she was cycling in intense heat in Ibiza – on a health kick, ironically – when she fell. She died of a cerebral haemorrhage.

The late Nico

Intimations of mortality were pressing hard on Reed and Cale. Cale had been prompted by artist Julian Schnabel to construct a musical tribute to the Factory legacy. After some months' groundwork, he approached his partner-in-crime from younger wilder days: it made sense. Reed, for once exhibiting good grace, was pleased to throw himself into the project (in fact, he ended up dominating it).

But first, Lou built *New York*. Momentum was again to gather around his recording career. He collaborated with salsa star Ruben Blades on his first English language album, adding acerbic lyrics and producing, and turned up on his soon-to-be bass player Rob Wasserman's album *Duets*, performing Frank Sinatra's "One For My Baby" passably well. He appeared in the Keanu Reeves flick *Permanent Record* (again as a rock star) and gave it the rocky number "Something Happened". Then, considering RCA to be to blame for the failure of *Mistrial*, he signed to Seymour Stein's Sire label, then the hottest indie crossover stable (though owned by Warner). He'd seen the label achieve credible success with the likes of Talking Heads and the Ramones (not to mention rising star Madonna), and as long as he promised to promote, they were glad to land the prestige and kudos of his name. They also had the smarts to market it efficiently. Reed was to tour the next album diligently.

"I don't know why people give me record deals," he wondered. "I think they break even, or even make a few bucks… I'm a cult figure, but I do sell some records." It turned out that *New York* was his best seller since *Sally Can't Dance*.

Teaming up with guitarist Mike Rathke, a friend of Sylvia's who he'd jammed with several times without Rathke feeling the need to be intimidated, and calling back Wasserman on bass and Fred Maher on drums, he worked on a set of new songs. And worked and worked. Through the latter half of 1988 (while at the same time he and Cale began writing the *Songs For Drella* project) they recorded: before that Reed had been over his lyrics countless times, tightening, focusing, adding and subtracting. If he'd offered up lazy work in the early to mid-'80s, he was to see the decade out as dedicated to his lyrical craft as he had once been to flamboyant statements and self-abuse. He slaved long hours over his word processor, remembering what he'd been taught by Delmore Schwartz, by reading Burroughs and Selby. *New York* was to be possibly his literary pinnacle. Many will argue that it's a great album, period. Its music is chiefly old-school rock, a four-piece band ignoring fashion and driving down the middle. Reed enjoys playing guitar very much, and often says so. But if *New York* is a great record, it's because of its literary merits, its intricate, uncensored news reports of a city's shadows and sleaze. It's John Dos Passos with passion. *Taxi Driver* with the pedal to the metal.

"I'm pretty upset about what's going on in New York City after eight years of Reagan. This government's been picking on all the people who can't defend themselves, and it's passed so far into the surreal now that you can't even satirise it." Even so, Reed succeeded. *New York* is Reed's real stab at a novel, his real walk on the wild side. It's an epic movie and an extended poem. Musically conservative, its strength lies in Reed's love of words and his new-found, hard-won ability to paint pictures that weren't self-portraits. "My first real record for years," he called it. "This is the absolute first time an album has actually come out the way I heard it in my head. I've objected to a lot of things in my time, but these days I'm doing something about it."

In *The Times*, David Sinclair wrote, "If Bob Dylan was plugged into the Eighties the way he was plugged into the Sixties, perhaps he could have come up with a commentary on the times to match this. Right now it's hard to think of anyone who has come close." And *Rolling Stone*'s Anthony De Curtis was equally effusive in his praise: "*New York*, at nearly an hour… is fierce poetic journalism, a reportage of surreal horror in which the unyielding force of actual circumstance continually threatens to overwhelm the ordering power of art. Reed, of course, is no stranger to unhinging scenes of squalor. On his inestimably influential early albums with the Velvet Underground, and through much of his solo work in the Seventies, Reed cast a cold eye on virtually every manner of human excess. But times have changed, and Reed's attitudes have changed with them. A walk on the sexually undifferentiated wild side is no longer simply an outrageous means of spitting in the face of the bourgeoisie, but a potentially fatal journey." For all the music's run-of-the-mill rock shapes, the lyrics merit such fervour.

It'd be glib to remark that the deaths of Warhol and Nico galvanised Reed, even if his next two albums were preoccupied with mortality. But writing *New York* – so good he named it once – brought the artist in him back to life.

"But remember that the city is a funny place," he'd advised, back on *Coney Island Baby*. "Something like a circus or a sewer." The metropolis of his new opus was Sodom and Gomorrah.

ROMEO HAD JULIETTE

"Caught between the twisted stars, the plotted lines, the faulty map that brought Columbus to New York…" With one of the most oft-quoted opening lines of his entire output Reed announces his intentions as a chronicler of the decaying ideals of the fantasy city, as a Theodore Dreiser watching mankind struggle against destiny and futility. Romance is dead and "Manhattan's sinking like a rock into the filthy Hudson". Guns, drugs, good intentions gone sour – it's a Shakespeare tragedy, it's the fall of Rome. For the first time in years, Reed is burning not fiddling.

HALLOWEEN PARADE

A comparatively jaunty *Transformer*-style shuffle underscores a portrayal of the Gay Pride parade past Christopher Street. The costumes are as defiantly colourful as ever, as in earlier Reed songs, but this year the fear of Aids, and the media's confused hostility towards it, permeates the atmosphere. Certain familiar (to Reed) faces are missing, presumed dead. "See you next year," he concludes with optimism so ironic it's pessimism.

DIRTY BLVD.

"Another contemporary tale of New York…" Reed writes on the *NYC Man* sleeve notes, making a special case for it. "That song, of all the songs, was incredibly hard to write, that very simple chord thing. That was one of the hardest things I ever had to work on. It's just three chords and the pattern was really hard to get." It's just a "Sweet Jane" kind of riff, simple but effective and beautifully adapted by the band, so why he makes such a big deal of it is baffling: however, lyrically the album really kicks in here. It was the show-horse single, released to promote the album on radio rather than in any hope of a "hit". The days of hit singles were behind Reed now, as they were, in an evolving marketplace, behind most '60s/'70s rock icons. (A certain

version of "Perfect Day" was to freakishly buck the trend, about which more later.)

We'd have to quote the entire lyric to do it justice: it's a clear-eyed piece of social vitriol. How the American Dream has corroded. "Give me your tired, your poor, I'll piss on 'em – that's what the Statue Of Bigotry says." Dion wanders through some backing vocals, and at the end "Pedro" can only wish he could "disappear, and fly, fly away"…

ENDLESS CYCLE

For all the literacy, you begin to wonder here if the musical backdrop is going to even try to be more than functional. But the country-ish chops and slides serve to lull us into a false sense of security before the next track's heavy stomp. It's a shame "Vicious Circle" on *Rock And Roll Heart* lacked the poetry glimpsed here though, in another analysis of the sins of the parents. "The truth is they're happier when they're in pain/In fact that's why they got married."

THERE IS NO TIME

Rawk! Screeching feedback-laden guitars and heads-down no-frills drums in a CBGB's-style garage boogie. One of the few tracks that couldn't be dismissed as bland midlife plod-rock were the lyrics removed. "This is no time for phony rhetoric…"

LAST GREAT AMERICAN WHALE

Moby Dick it ain't. Mo Tucker rumbles through some timpani-like drums on this (and the closing number). "Jeez, what a great title," exclaimed Reed. "Give me a good title and I'm home free. I wrote the first version and it was horrible, but I'm not interested in whether it's good or bad, I just want the thing written out. Then I can go someplace with it." Part mythical, part naturalistic, it criticises America's abuse of the environment and of Native Americans. Ahead of his time by a few years, Reed

observes: "Americans don't care for much of anything/Land and water the least… they'll shit in a river, dump battery acid in a stream…" He closes bleakly with a line "my painter friend Donald said to me" (and a line which John Mellencamp had previously deployed): "Stick a fork in their ass, turn them over, they're done…"

BEGINNING OF A GREAT ADVENTURE

Adding to the debate of why you'd want to bring a baby into this world, Reed carves out a fine slice of what is, for this album, light relief. Over walking-jazz bass lines and Maher's flicks and bumps, Reed recites a list of possible names for his offspring – these range amusingly from Bogart and Bono to Marlon and The Glob. "I'd need a damn computer to keep track of all these names." It might be fun, he muses, to have a kid he could kick around, to keep him company when he's a "wizened, toothless old clod". The track's full of both good jokes and bad forebodings (given the author's own dysfunctional upbringing). When Reed and Sylvia did split up in the early '90s, it was said that his reluctance to have kids was a factor. Maybe he'd had enough great adventures of his own.

BUSLOAD OF FAITH

You need such a busload to get by, because, he says, you can't depend on anything except that the worst will happen. But he's not whining: he's collating evidence, he's thought this through. Old-school riffing and a meaty grinding riff, but another great track to read. All those years of grafting at private poetry had paid off.

SICK OF YOU

A bumpkin trot backs another gob of rationally misanthropic bile. Getting it in the ass this time are the President (whose head has gone missing), the Ayatollah, Rudy Giuliani, and NASA, who've blown up the moon. Reed takes the macabre surreal

flights he dabbled in on his first two solo albums and makes them count, makes them hit specific targets. He's heard the news and it's grim listening. He's a better protest singer than he's ever been.

HOLD ON

"Ha ha ha ha!" it begins. Well, by now, it's the only response left. More graphic reportage from the edge ensues, until the twin guitars melt down. Topically, "it'll take more than the Angels or Iron Mike Tyson to heal this bloody breach". Murderous moments frozen in time. Great writing. The phrase "hold on" has rarely provided less reassurance.

GOOD EVENING MR. WALDHEIM

Confused, confusing politics, which assault both Jesse Jackson and Louis Farrakhan over nondescript Chuck Berry licks. Jackson and his followers were deeply insulted. If this was incendiary, the harrowing tale of Vietnam's legacy that followed was even more so.

XMAS IN FEBRUARY

Laid-back music, heart-attack lyrics. Vietnam vets return home to find home isn't a place of comfort. Wounded, broke, neglected, their friends in body bags, they struggle to land menial jobs and survive domestic crack-ups. They live American lives that have no second act, and their first was a violent travesty. Xmas in February? You can't find that anywhere, no matter how resilient you are.

STRAWMAN

A full-on rocker, and musically the album's most in-your-face piece, with Reed hollering like urgent sandpaper. The "straw man" is America, is the symbol of authority, arguably well meaning, unarguably destructive, "going straight to the devil". A litany of rhetoric, Reed demanding to know if we really "need" the things prioritised by government and the media, from faulty space shuttles to

"another self-righteous rock singer, whose nose he says has led him straight to God". The USA, he appears to be summarising, is going to reap just what it sows. And that could be the whirlwind. Only a miracle can save Gotham City now.

DIME STORE MYSTERY

An epilogue, of sorts, dedicated "to Andy – honey". It refers directly to Warhol's funeral at St Patrick's – "tomorrow… the bells will ring for you" – and in a foreshadowing of *Songs For Drella* and *Magic And Loss* Reed sighs, "I wish I hadn't thrown away my time on so much Human and so much less Divine." Prior to this the imagery speaks, with allusion to Scorsese's controversial film *The Last Temptation Of Christ*, of a figure on the cross, "banged and battered, skewered and bleeding". If the wealth of reference is impressive – Descartes and Hegel also get namechecks – I've yet to meet anyone who clearly understands what Reed is trying to say here. If such lofty subject matter is a "dime store mystery", is he belittling it? Is the song getting to grips with religion, or with

Warhol's death? One is left unsure, to say the least.

On the other hand, it's sonically the most interesting, intriguing thing on the record, with Mo Tucker again involved as the musicians break out of their four-square regulations. The piece follows a faulty map, then, but is brave to even approach "the mysteries of life".

"For a while, I felt a little self-compelled to write Lou Reed-type of songs. I should have understood that a Lou Reed song was anything that I wanted to write about."

With *New York* Reed had finally nailed down his own map of the hassles of the streets. What ran through them, not through his veins. If it was a pity that his musical ambitions were becoming reductive – "you can't beat two guitars, bass, drum," he boasted on the album sleeve – his muses were firing again. Another phrase from his sleeve notes – "It's meant to be listened to in one sitting… as though it were a book or a movie" – gave a clear indication of where his ambitions now lay. In the realm of the highbrow.

SONGS FOR DRELLA April **(1990)**

SMALLTOWN ❥ **OPEN HOUSE** ❥ STYLE IT TAKES ❥ **WORK** ❥ TROUBLE WITH CLASSICISTS ❥ **STARLIGHT** ❥ FACES AND NAMES ❥ **IMAGES** ❥ SLIP AWAY (A WARNING) ❥ **IT WASN'T ME** ❥ I BELIEVE NOBODY BUT YOU ❥ **A DREAM** ❥ FOREVER CHANGED ❥ **HELLO IT'S ME** Produced: Lou Reed and John Cale **Recorded:** Sigma Sound, New York City **Musicians:** Lou Reed (vocals, guitars); John Cale (vocals, keyboards, viola).

Not strictly a Reed solo album but a duet with John Cale, initially commissioned by the Brooklyn Academy Of Music, so we have to heartlessly skim over it here. The very fact that they were collaborating again was the story. As a tribute to Warhol – an obvious act of atonement on Reed's part – it's a pompous, sexless piece of music. Still, it was sincere, and drew attention, and helped bring about the brief mixed blessing of a Velvets reunion.

Reed and Cale had performed a rough draft live as far back as January 1989, before Reed had to focus on the release and promotion of *New York*. He toured the States and Europe, with Mo Tucker supporting in the States in August. Unfortunately the later tour had to be cut short when Lou broke his ankle falling down some stairs. He did however manage cameos on albums by idol-turned-buddy Dion and *Street Hassle* devotees Simple Minds. Cale and Reed premiered *Songs For Drella* at the Brooklyn Academy Of Music on 30 November 1989, and the finished album came out the next year. At the Brooklyn shows, Mo Tucker joined the pair onstage one night.

As the track titles might suggest, it ends up being more about Reed's words than the music, whether that had been originally intended or not. On the sleeve, Cale magnanimously declared that it was "a collaboration, the second Lou and I have completed since 1965. I must say that although I think he did most of the work, he has allowed me to keep a position of dignity in the process. It therefore remains, as intended, a tribute to someone whose inspiration and generosity offered over the years is

now remembered with much love and affection." Later, though, Cale was to confess, "Recording *Drella* with Lou was very difficult. There was a lot of banging heads... never dull, but I wouldn't want to go through it again."

Reed said, "I was disturbed by all these evil books presenting Andy Warhol as just a piece of fluff. I wanted to show the Andy I knew. It's very ordered and specific work." In truth you could argue that the stately, sombre *Songs For Drella* misses the point and spirit of Warhol by as great a distance as is conceivable.

The nickname "Drella" was a cross between Cinderella and Dracula. The album's tales talked with both tender and tough love of characters from the Factory era and "scene" such as Truman Capote, Salvador Dali, Edie Sedgwick, Viva, Ingrid Polk, Joe Alexandra ("Little Joe"), Baby Jane Holzer, the late Ondine, Valerie Solanis and photographer Billy Name. It eulogised Andy's work ethic, and found Reed owning up to some imperfect judgement. "Andy... I wish I'd talked to you more when you were alive/I thought you were self-assured when you acted shy." Even here, Reed couldn't resist sticking up for his own side of things in the ego-fuelled afterthought "Hello It's Me". "Your diaries are not a worthy epitaph." Such subjective pettiness at least prevented the project from lapsing into mushy sentimentality.

Reed himself helpfully described it thus: "*Songs For Drella – A Fiction* is a brief musical look at the life of Andy Warhol and is entirely fictitious. We start with Andy growing up in 'Smalltown' – 'There's

The odd couple - Cale and Reed

no Michelangelo coming from Pittsburgh.' He comes to New York and follows the customs of 'Open House' both in his apartments and the Factory. 'It's a Czechoslovakia custom my mother passed on to me/The way to make friends Andy is to invite them up for tea.' He travels around the world and is, in his words, 'Forever Changed'. He knows the importance of people and money in the art world ('Style It Takes') and follows his primary work ethic, 'Work – the most important thing is work.' He can copy the classicists but feels 'the trouble with classicists, they look at a tree/That's all they see, they paint a tree …'

"Andy wished we all had the same 'Faces And Names'. He becomes involved with movies – 'Starlight'. He is interested in repetitive 'Images' – 'I love images worth repeating … see them with a different feeling.' The mortality rate at the Factory is rather high and some blame Andy – 'It wasn't me who shamed you …' The open house policy leads to him being shot ('I Believe'). He had been warned but a new, locked door approach to the Factory caused him to wonder, 'If I have to live in fear/Where will I get my ideas… will I slowly slip away?' One night he has 'A Dream'; his relationships change – 'A Nobody Like You'. He dies recovering from a gall bladder operation.

"Chocolates were his weakness. We miss him very much."

MAGIC AND LOSS January **(1992)**

DORITA – THE SPIRIT ❥ **WHAT'S GOOD – THE THESIS** ❥ POWER AND GLORY – THE SITUATION ❥ **MAGICIAN – INTERNALLY** ❥ SWORD OF DAMOCLES – EXTERNALLY ❥ **GOODBY MASS – IN A CHAPEL BODILY TERMINATION** ❥ CREMATION – ASHES TO ASHES ❥ **DREAMIN' – ESCAPE** ❥ NO CHANCE – REGRET ❥ **WARRIOR KING – REVENGE** ❥ HARRY'S CIRCUMCISION – REVERIE GONE ASTRAY ❥ **GASSED AND STOKED – LOSS** ❥ POWER AND GLORY part 2 – MAGIC, TRANSFORMATION ❥ **MAGIC AND LOSS – THE SUMMATION** Produced: Lou Reed and Mike Rathke

Recorded at: Magic Shop, New York City **Musicians:** Lou Reed (vocals, guitars); Mike Rathke (guitars); Rob Wasserman (upright bass); Michael Blair (drums, percussion); Little Jimmy Scott, Roger Moutenot (background vocals).

"**B**etween two Aprils I lost two friends/Between two Aprils magic and loss…"
Reviews for Reed's work were now uniformly favourable, though generally from reviewers who'd grown older alongside him. Younger fans were finding the "mature" material stilted, drab and worthy: *Magic And Loss*, perceived as a success both critically and commercially, left anyone under forty cold. Exhilarating it was not. The bespectacled and buttoned-up music, precise and poised, dripped like a tap. But it came dressed as High Art, and which reviewers seeing themselves as defenders of "the intelligence that would ingest rock" were brave enough to make comments concerning emperor's new clothes? The technical side of recording was of paramount importance to Reed now: he and Rathke spent longer mixing this album (the best part of a year) than recording it. In one interview he spoke at length of "the kind of tape you record on". (Is that hiss we hear or just zzzzz …?) Again, it's just interesting verse set to sketchy, functional sounds.

What else had Professor Reed been up to? He'd sung at Wembley Stadium in 1990 at the Nelson Mandela benefit show (two *New York* songs on acoustic guitar). He'd met Czech president (and Reed fan) Václav Havel, in the guise of interviewing him for *Rolling Stone* magazine. But as Reed spent most of the allotted time talking about himself, the interview never ran. Another magazine, *Q*, had given him their Outstanding Achievement Award. The French government made him a knight of the order of arts and letters, and RCA released a haughty retrospective box set, *Between Thought And Expression*. Is it possible that all these highfalutin' pats on the back led Reed to believe he was the world's greatest writer rather than a once-great rock star who could write better than most rock stars?

Magic And Loss concerned itself with death and absent friends. It was dedicated to (and told of) Jerome Pomus, aka "Doc", a songwriter friend who'd written hits for Elvis Presley and Dion & the Belmonts among others, and "Rotten Rita", a speed-freak who clean-living Lou had known since back in the '60s. Both had died recently. "These were people who were inspiring me right up to the last minute," said Lou. "Within a short period, two of the most important people in my life died from cancer, so the piece is about friendship and how it transforms things… But it would have been even worse not to have known them at all. That's the *Magic And Loss* deal."

It's revealing that Reed refers to it as a "piece". "Not the stuff hits are made of," observed one reviewer. "What it lacks in pop appeal is more than made up for by emotional impact," argued another. "With arrangements so skeletal they're barely noticeable, the album stakes everything on its songs. Reed makes them work with sly melodic twists and a well-framed narrative, assuring that we not only understand his emotional turmoil, but share in it. Which, in the end, makes this a perfect modern blues: heartbreaking, thought-provoking, involving as life."

We do not share. It is not involving. Credit Reed – a self-professed insomniac at the time – for his courage in bringing Big Themes to the album charts, but in doing so he sacrificed any of the energising power of music. *Berlin* had been morbid, but thrillingly so. He was the earnest, bookish literature student of his youth, only without the nocturnal, let-your-hair-down parties. "Death is one of the great themes," he proclaimed, and, "I know what it's like to be outside. I know what it's like to have an unhappy childhood. I delineate people because either I identify with them or I think they deserve their moment in the sun."

Rolling Stone's David Fricke concurred with Reed's own assessment of the record's merits, calling it his best since *The Blue Mask* (not hard outside of *New York*). "[It's] a stunning consummation of that album's naked guitar clamour, the hushed chapel intimacy of the third Velvet Underground album and the barbed reportorial vitality of Reed's best songwriting. He offers no great moral revelations, no happy ever after, just big questions and some basic horse sense." "Vitality"? Did he say "vitality"?

The album reeked of loss, but not of magic. Doleful and self-reverential, it forced you to be polite and listen, but you resented the imposition later. It was a nanny state of a record. The attendant tour went too far: Reed had the audiences sit in silence, and they were barred from drinking, smoking or even talking. Comparing the work to Beethoven's Fifth, he played the album from start to end, and even Seymour Stein protested: "Woah! Is this about cancer?" Reed would vehemently argue that "people who like that record are people who have been visited by the real world. I suppose there's classical music, like a Mass or something, but this is different. Once I started writing it, I couldn't stop."

"Between two Aprils I lost two friends/Between two Aprils magic and loss …"

A pity. What never occurs to Reed is that, in mourning, it may not cross our minds to put a Lou Reed album on. And even if it did, hey, we've already got the million-times-more-arresting *Berlin*. If we want a sad song, if we want *the* sad song, we know where to go. Lou Reed, prone as he was to talking up the "depth" of *Magic And Loss*, referred to this the closest descendant of *Berlin*, but nobody for a single moment thought it was Mary Queen Of Scots.

SET THE TWILIGHT REELING (1996)

EGG CREAM ❥ **NYC MAN** ❥ FINISH LINE ❥ **TRADE IN** ❥ HANG ON TO YOUR EMOTIONS ❥ **SEX WITH YOUR PARENTS PART 2** ❥ HOOKYWOOKY ❥ **THE PROPOSITION** ❥ ADVENTURER ❥ **RIPTIDE** ❥ SET THE TWILIGHT REELING ❥ **Produced:** Lou Reed **Recorded at:** The Roof, New York; The Magic Shop, New York **Musicians:** Lou Reed (vocals, all guitars); Fernando Saunders (bass, backing vocals); Tony "Thunder" Smith (drums, backing vocals); Laurie Anderson (backing vocals); Oliver Lake, J.D. Parran and Russell Gunn Jr (horns); Minu Cinelu (percussion); Roy Bittan (piano).

The most remarkable and unexpected aspect of the years before Reed's next solo effort was of course the re-formation of the Velvet Underground, but this – a great idea on paper – was a disaster in reality, doing nothing to bolster the power of the myth. We can only mention it in passing here, but it was perhaps a mercy when it fizzled out. The European shows dragged; the best efforts of the other three to rub along with Lou were doused by his control-freak tendencies and bitterness. He envied and coveted Cale's intellectual reputation.

American fans were offended by the lack of any US shows. The flimsy new material was perfunctory and meretricious, and one decision – to support U2 in Italian stadiums – was plain bizarre. As Lou's manager, the domineering Sylvia Reed ran roughshod over the feelings of Cale, Morrison and Tucker, who she saw as a mere backing band. Reed shrieked at the others bossily onstage, within earshot of audiences: Cale was less than impressed. When, in a *Melody Maker* interview, Allan Jones inquired of Cale if Reed had taken to being "uncommonly democratic", Cale replied, "Lou, democratic? Let's not go too far. Put it this way – if he thinks I'm going to turn up and play 'Walk On The Wild Side', he's going to be very disappointed." Max Bell in *Vox* told of Reed silently staring out the other musicians. In *NME*, Roger Morton retained a level of critical detachment: "Four chronologically advanced musicians performing basic, broody adolescent rock songs with about as much passion as a quartet of railway announcers makes for a strange spectacle. Sawing away at his violin, the curate-like Cale deports himself with bizarre solemnity… and Reed croaks on… the whole thing has the deadening atmosphere of an angst-pop master class."

The Reeds' own marriage was now in aggressive decline, and their separation (and Reed's sacking of Sylvia as manager) became inevitable. Blame and

recriminations flew back and forth. A painful and messy divorce ensued. One wonders if Reed any longer cares for all those lyrics that eulogise her very name. The fact remains that she made the one-time rock'n'roll animal a valid proposition to the music industry at large, a durable brand name capable of reliably making money. Even if the juice and spontaneity was gone. His new love was experimental artist/musician Laurie Anderson, best known to many for the freak hit "O Superman".

Whereas once Reed had been eager to spill the beans on his private life, now that was very much a no-go zone for journalists. So he continued to speak of recording techniques and studio gadgetry. *Set The Twilight Reeling* felt like an exorcism, a cathartic letting off of steam: after the crushing earnestness of his last few releases, it cracks a joke or two, yells a bit, throws its toys out of the pram. A good thing, in theory. But it's not a good record, just a moderately entertaining one. It's Bowie's *Tin Machine* without the sharp suits. There are goofy nostalgic lyrics ("Egg

Cream"), over-the-top attempts to prove he can still shock ("Sex With Your Parents" – actually an unsubtle dig at right-wing Republicans), a dedication to the recently deceased Sterling Morrison ("Finish Line"), and a stodgy stab at echoing Dylan Thomas's immortal "Do not go gentle into that good night" on the title track. "I accept the new-found man and set the twilight reeling." This finale is littered with truly terrible "poetry".

Of "NYC Man", a conciliatory rock hymn to the city, he said, "Its music is such a New York sound. A romantic sound. This is what I hear when I think of Manhattan Island." The title was borrowed for his next compilation album. It was as if he wanted to assure New York that he loved it really, and wasn't it the New Yorker's prerogative to bitch and moan about the city he loved?

Elsewhere there were love notes to Laurie Anderson. On "Trade In", for instance, "I met a woman with a thousand faces and I want to make her my wife." "A great song," he later nodded to *Uncut* magazine. "Once in a while I get a song like that and no one notices. I love the lyrics, everything. It really captured that… kind of… 'Oh, you sweet thing'."

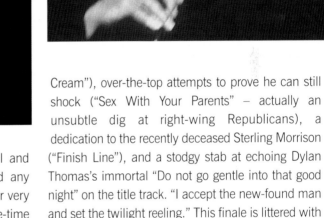

PERFECT NIGHT:
LIVE IN LONDON
(1998)

I'LL BE YOUR MIRROR ❥ PERFECT DAY ❥ **THE KIDS** ❥ VICIOUS ❥ **BUSLOAD OF FAITH** ❥ KICKS ❥ **TALKING BOOK** ❥ INTO THE DIVINE ❥ **CONEY ISLAND BABY** ❥ NEW SENSATIONS ❥ **WHY DO YOU TALK** ❥ RIPTIDE ❥ **THE ORIGINAL WRAPPER** ❥ SEX WITH YOUR PARENTS ❥ **DIRTY BLVD.** Produced: Lou Reed and Mike Rathke **Recorded:** Royal Festival Hall, London **Musicians:** Lou Reed (guitar, vocals); Mike Rathke (guitar); Fernando Saunders (bass, vocals); Tony "Thunder" Smith (drums).

Live in London, from a 3 July 1997 show at the South Bank's annual Meltdown Festival. The curator that year? Laurie Anderson. It's sedate and considered, proud of its pristine sound – you couldn't get further away from *Rock'n'Roll Animal*. On the sleeve Reed drones on about "purity" of acoustics, how it's all about "me and the guys in the band". Oh he's such a good ol' boy. Given its dryness, the album's very decent, with a healthy cross section of material chosen, from the unexpectedly brave ("Kicks", "Coney Island Baby") to the blatant plugs (anything from *Set The Twilight Reeling*) to a devil-may-care funky fling through "The Original Wrapper". But it's all about "Perfect Day", sung lovingly and without irony here.

The strangest thing had happened. The BBC, in its surreal wisdom, had used the 1972 song as its new promotional anthem. To advertise its diversity, the Corporation had grabbed an array of celebrities to warble a line each: Bowie, Bono, Pavarotti, various teeny-pop stars, the valid and the vacuous, even Reed himself. It captured the popular imagination (possibly not everybody grasped the finer nuances) and, as a by-public-demand charity record, soared to Number One. Lou Reed was now that nice man who wrote the pretty tune about happiness which everyone and their neighbour knew. OK, stranger things *have* happened. But only in the world of Lou Reed. His week was still beating our year.

ECSTASY

May **(2000)**

PARANOIA KEY OF E ➤ **MYSTIC CHILD** ➤ MAD ➤ **ECSTASY** ➤ MODERN DANCE ➤ **TATTERS** ➤ FUTURE FARMERS OF AMERICA ➤ **TURNING TIME AROUND** ➤ WHITE PRISM ➤ **ROCK MINUET** ➤ BATON ROUGE ➤ **LIKE A POSSUM** ➤ ROUGE ➤ **SEX WITH YOUR PARENTS** ➤ DIRTY BLVD

Produced: Lou Reed and Hal Willner **Recorded:** Sear Sound Studios, New York **Musicians:** Lou Reed (vocals, guitar, percussion on "White Prism"); Mike Rathke (guitar); Fernando Saunders (bass, backing vocals); Tony Smith (drums, backing vocals); Don Alias (percussion on "Ecstasy"); Laurie Anderson (electric violin on "Rock Minuet" and "Rouge"); Steven Bernstein (trumpet, horn arrangements); Jane Scranton (cellos); Paul Shapiro (tenor sax); Doug Wiseman (tenor and baritone sax).

While the tired phrase "a return to form" is by now rendered almost unworkable by Reed's unpredictability, *Ecstasy* is happily deranged. It was acclaimed by *Uncut* as "a work of anger and beauty, his strongest since 1992" – which, if you think about it, is a clever way of saying at least it's better than *Set The Twilight Reeling*. What's best about it is that Reed seems to be getting personal again, discussing relationships and emotions rather than abstracts. There had been hints on its predecessor that he was prepared to let his guard slip a little once again, that he might let us catch a glimpse of the man behind the shades. But this went further, exposed more. *Uncut*'s Nick Johnstone reckoned that "If *New York* was a great album about everything that surrounded Lou Reed, then *Ecstasy* is a great album about everything inside Lou Reed." Which is where we want him to look. As an aesthetic as opposed to a socialist.

If greatness is beyond it, there are some intensely juicy moments. He'll never again exhibit the utter lack of self-consciousness that once made him catch fire, but it does hook your attention. "The thing about 'Ecstasy'," he has said, referring to the cryptic title track, "is that it just has a killer guitar riff. I think of that riff the way I think of the 'Sweet Jane' riff. Once in a while you get a really good guitar lick… I get a kick out of that." Of the contrasting "Rock Minuet", he has said, "That's a light-hearted song about a man and his father. I like the idea of trying to revisit *Oedipus Rex*. I

really believe this is one of the greatest songs I've ever done of that type. It's up there with 'Street Hassle'. It's… a real head trip, a really serious examination of feeling for your father. Some people will understand it; other people will be actively upset by it."

Like "White Prism", it's as graphic as the work of his heyday. There's the serious philosophical globetrotting comedy of "Modern Dance". "Paranoia Key Of E" is "just having fun". "Tatters" dissects broken relationships: "I suppose we could all say that nothing of it matters/But still it's sad to see everything in tatters." "Baton Rouge" pines for a conventional heterosexual youth he never had. "It was the hardest song to record on the whole album. It's hilarious… then it takes a turn, and it's wistful." And then there's the extraordinary "Like A Possum"…

At no less than eighteen minutes long, it's a monolith. "We would just play the riff for hours and hours… hours of doing that just did something wonderful. Then it was just a way of figuring out a way to sing to it…" Orchestral, speculative and in Reed's own words, "monumental", it contains lines which will be welcome meat and drink to long-term Reed aficionados. Such as: "I got a hole in my heart the size of a truck/It won't be filled by a one night fuck." Or: "You know me I like to dance a lot/With different selves who cancel out one another/… One likes muscles, oil and dirt/The other likes women with the butt that hurts."

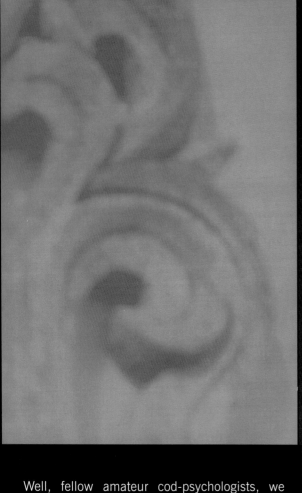

Well, fellow amateur cod-psychologists, we haven't had this much fun in years of Reed! Of course it's not "him", he's "telling a story", but he's telling the kind of story we used to consider him the go-to guy for. After a decade of sanity and sanctimony from him, this is shocking only in that it's such a reversal. It transpired that Reed was now a full-blown insomniac, pacing around and writing these songs at five in the morning. Our hero was once again a creature of the night (all through the night), and his work was so much the better, and franker, and looser, for it.

THE RAVEN   (2003)

BROADWAY SONG ❯ **THE TELL-TALE HEART** ❯ VANISHING ACT ❯ **I WANNA KNOW (THE PIT AND THE PENDULUM)** ❯ HOP FROG ❯ **GUARDIAN ANGEL** ❯ THE CONQUEROR WORM ❯ **OLD POE** ❯ THE VALLEY OF UNREST ❯ **THE FALL OF THE HOUSE OF USHER** ❯ THE BED ❯ **PERFECT DAY** ❯ THE RAVEN... and many more... **Produced:** Lou Reed and Hal Willner **Recorded:** Sear Sound Studios, New York; Clinton Recording, New York; Cove City Sound Studios, Long Island; The Roof, New York; Looking Glass Studio, New York. **Musicians:** Lou Reed, Mike Rathke, Fernando Saunders, Tony Smith, plus many guests including David Bowie, Steve Buscemi, Willem Dafoe, Amanda Plummer, Kate Valk, Fisher Stevens, Kate and Anna McGarrigle, Ornette Coleman, The Blind Boys of Alabama, Antony, Laurie Anderson.

For every Yin, a Yang. For every fascinating Lou Reed album nowadays, a car crash. *The Raven* is a concept double album, a piece of performance art, a kind of soundtrack to a theatrical production. And out of context, as "just" music, it's horrendous. It's all about Edgar Allan Poe, one of Reed's heroes, and it's po-faced in the extreme. It's practically a test case in what happens when pretentious ageing rock gods get ideas above their station. Be grateful it's "only" a double... Reed slings together new material, redrafts of old classics, poetry readings and gauche cameos from a host of star names. One doesn't doubt they all love the work of Edgar Allan Poe. One does doubt that this does the literary titan's reputation any favours. It's too precious to be gothic; too overblown to catch any feeling of nocturnal mystery... it's a record that few people will play all the way through twice. Not many critics were found ravin' (ha ha) about it.

The seeds of the project had been sown in *Time Rocker* (everything suggests *Ecstasy* was a necessary reaction to and psychically welcome release from its constraints). *Time Rocker* was, Reed wrote in the foreword to his book of collected lyrics, *Pass Thru Fire*, "a play that I did with Robert Wilson. We were interested in transcending time, passing through it and its various boundaries and worlds." Certainly *The Raven* seems to last beyond forever. "We didn't have a rented car," adds Reed

helpfully, "but a time-travelling fish." Uh... right.

Some of those songs made the switch, along with "Perfect Day" and "The Bed". Reed's now enamoured of the cello, and of falsetto vocalist Antony (both of whom featured on his next tour, and the subsequent *Animal Serenade* document). And there's a lot of spoken word on *The Raven*. Luminaries like Willem Dafoe and Steve Buscemi line up to recite Poe. David Bowie – presumably, with the old sparring partners both living in New York now, bygones are bygones – sings the one concise track, "Hop Frog", with jolly abandon. Reed sings the big but not grand finale "Guardian Angel", taking seven minutes to make a simple point. Julian Schnabel takes expensive cover shots of Lou wielding an Excalibur-style sword. Or, more accurately, of Lou failing to wield it because it's too heavy for him to lift. The pompousness is risible.

Which one of Reed's "selves" turned up here? The ridiculously earnest self-regarding lecturer, seeking literary props by association. Making love to high art by proxy.

We should at least allow his revealing sleeve notes to offer some degree of explanation. There's an element of identification. "For sure Edgar Allan Poe is that most classical of American writers – a writer more peculiarly attuned to our new century's heartbeat than he ever was to his own.

Obsessions, paranoia, wilful acts of self-destruction surround us constantly. Though we age we still hear the cries of those for whom the attraction to mournful chaos is monumental. I have reread and rewritten Poe to ask the very same questions again. Who am I? Why am I drawn to what I should not? I have wrestled with this thought innumerable times: the impulse of destructive desire – the desire for self-mortification. To my mind Poe is father to William Burroughs and Hubert Selby. I am forever fitting their blood to my melodies..."

And later: "Why do we have a passion for exactly the wrong thing? What do we mean by 'wrong'? I became enamoured of Poe once again, and when given the opportunity to bring him to life through words and music, text and dance, why, I leapt at it. I surged towards it like a Rottweiler chasing a bloody bone." Lou goes on to report that he saw

Reed combines with Willem Dafoe (top, with Wim Wenders) and old friend David Bowie (bottom) for The Raven

the early performances at the Thalia Theatre in Germany (who had commissioned him to write this) "where the thrill of its existence only made me hunger more ardently for its American counterpart, its final rewrite". That "yearning" was fulfilled by this production, and the musicians, whose gifts he praises. (Notably, whereas everyone else gets gushing adjectives in front of their names, one just gets a curt "D. Bowie".) All this formed for Lou "a universe of sound I'd only dreamed of". "I thank them all from the bottom of my heart and reel with happiness at the CD's existence."

The rest of us simply reel. "This is a record," concludes Lou, "made of love." So somebody loves it then.

ANIMAL SERENADE (2003)

ADVICE (SWEET JANE) ❯ SMALLTOWN ❯ **TELL IT TO YOUR HEART** ❯ MEN OF GOOD FORTUNE ❯ **HOW DO YOU THINK IT FEELS** ❯ VANISHING ACT ❯ **ECSTASY** ❯ THE DAY JOHN KENNEDY DIED ❯ **STREET HASSLE** ❯ THE BED ❯ **REVIEN** ❯ CHERIE ❯ **VENUS IN FURS** ❯ DIRTY BLVD. ❯ **SUNDAY MORNING** ❯ ALL TOMORROW'S PARTIES ❯ **CALL ON ME** ❯ THE RAVEN ❯ **SET THE TWILIGHT REELING** ❯ CANDY SAYS ❯ **HEROIN** and many more **Produced:** Lou Reed and Fernando Saunders **Recorded:** The Wiltern Theater, Los Angeles **Musicians:** Lou Reed (vocals, guitar); Mike Rathke (guitar, guitar synth, ztar); Fernando Saunders (bass, guitar, vocals, piccolo bass, Roland drum); Antony (background vocals), Jane Scarpantoni (cello).

Yet another live double from Sister Ray Enterprises, embalming the tour of over sixty shows which took in the US, Europe, Canada, Australia and Japan. And, leaning as it does towards the very early or very late Reed work, it's of minimal consequence or charisma. Taped at LA's Wiltern Theater, it's pristine in sound (the way Lou likes it), lacking in grit. The songs are arranged to benefit the cellos, the absence of percussive instruments and Antony's unintentionally creepy falsetto chimings, with Lou occasionally talking up the pomp and ceremony of it all... ah the purity... but only rarely cracking wise. It's hard to believe this pussycat is the same tiger who gave us *Rock'n'Roll Animal* or the hellcat who rattled out *Take No Prisoners*. The *Berlin* songs are rendered bland, "Street Hassle" sounds filleted. Lou's ten-minute reading of "The Raven" is distinctly uncalled for. There's even a Fernando Saunders solo track ("Revien Cherie"). It's all very ... respectable.See the interview at the beginning of this book, however, for Lou's views on it.

Arguably, among Reed's peers, only Patti Smith has found an exciting way to combine the urgency and energy of youthful naïveté with the compensations of mature knowledge and pacing. Reed is still capable, one hopes and feels of tapping into his various personas for creativity, the 2004 remix of "Satellite of Love" is a success on most levels, but here he sounds like he's in his rocking chair, smug in the belief that his songs are strong enough to do the talking and testifying for him. Many of them are, but not through these snoozing versions, which are irreverent in all the wrong ways.

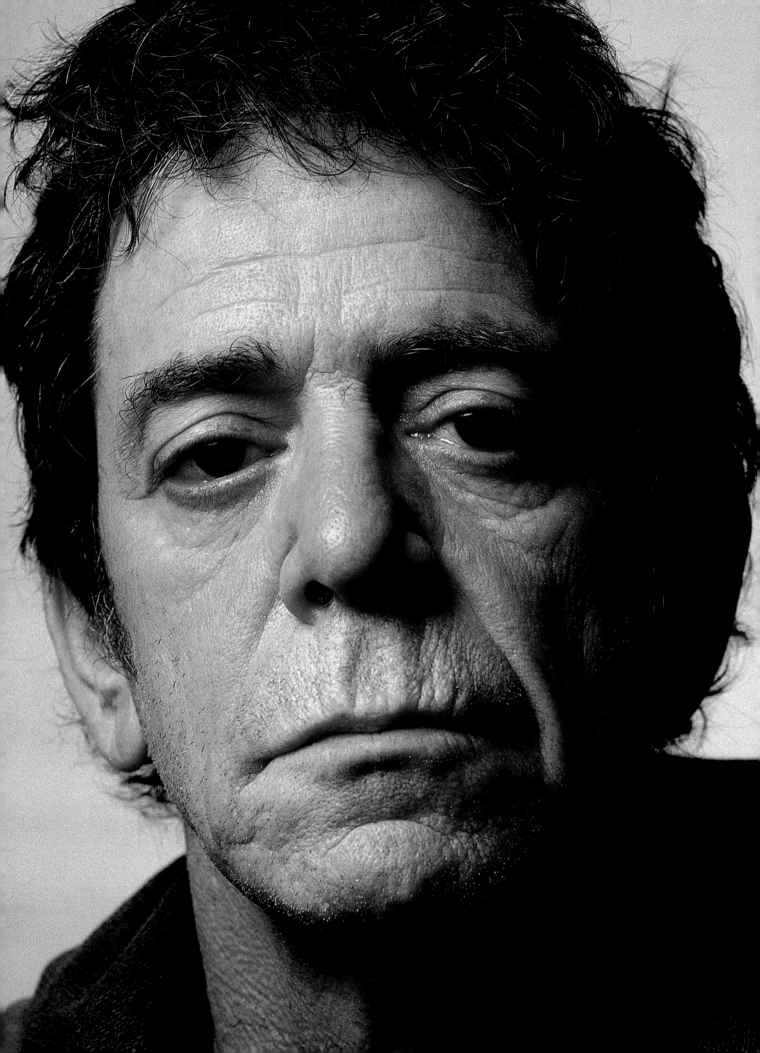

Lou Reed may not be the force he was - in truth he's probably close to standing for everything he used to rail against - but let's not lose sight of the fact that, in his finest, most fiery, most incalculably influential bursts of magic, he took rock and roll to previously unscaled heights, previously unplumbed depths, and most points between. The New York City man was, while beside himself and trapped inside himself in the '70s... well, he was The Man. Which is where we came in...

Now he rarely loses his head. Perhaps he is much happier this way.

DISCOGRAPHY

SOLO ALBUMS

1972 *Lou Reed*

1972 *Transformer*

1973 *Berlin*

1974 *Rock'n'Roll Animal*

1974 *Sally Can't Dance*

1975 *Lou Reed Live*

1975 *Metal Machine Music*

1975 *Coney Island Baby*

1976 *Rock And Roll Heart*

1978 *Street Hassle*

1978 *Take No Prisoners*

1979 *The Bells*

1980 *Growing Up In Public*

1982 *The Blue Mask*

1982 *Legendary Hearts*

1984 *Live In Italy*

1984 *New Sensations*

1986 *Mistrial*

1989 *New York*

1990 *Songs For Drella* (with John Cale)

1992 *Magic And Loss*

1996 *Set The Twilight Reeling*

1998 *Perfect Night*

2000 *Ecstasy*

2003 *The Raven*

2004 *Animal Serenade*

DISPLAY D ENDS

RECOMMENDED COMPILATIONS

1997 *Walk On The Wild Side*

1980 *Rock'n'Roll Diary*

1989 *Retro*

1997 *Perfect Day*

1999 *The Very Best Of Lou Reed*

2003 *NYC Man*

THE VELVET UNDERGROUND ALBUMS (WHICH FEATURE REED)

1967 *The Velvet Underground And Nico*

1969 *White Light/White Heat*

1970 *Loaded*

1972 *Live At Max's Kansas City*

1972 *Velvet Underground*

1974 *Live 1969*

1985 *VU*

1986 *Another VU*

1989 *The Best Of The Velvet Underground*

1993 *Live MCMXCIII*

SOURCES & THANKS

Thanks to: *Lou Reed: The Biography* – Victor Bockris (Hutchinson)

Lou Reed: Growing Up In Public – Peter Doggett (Omnibus)

Lou Reed: Between The Lines – Michael Wrenn (Plexus)

Pass Thru Fire (The Collected Lyrics) – Lou Reed (Bloomsbury)

Thanks also to: Allan Jones, Andy Prevezer, Uncut.

PICTURE CREDITS

Angela Lubrano: 119

Camera Press: Nils Meilvang/Scanpix: 130-31

Corbis Images: 78-79; /Bettman: 55; /Christopher Felver: 105; /Allen Ginsberg: 51; /Lynn Goldsmith: 81, 85; /Jordan Kelly: 133; /John-Marshall Mantel:84; /Andrew Murray: 109; /Neal Preston: 74

Gerard Malanga: 4-5 , 12, 16-17, 26-27, 33, 36-37, 66, 77, 140; /Archives Malanga: 143; /Courtesy Gerard Malanga Collection: 2, 25

Getty Images: Hulton Archive: 117; /Laura Levine/Time Life Pictures: 120; /Lawrence Lucier: 128; /Robin Platzer: 97

Picture Desk: The Kobal Collection/Court Productions: 67

Redferns: Paul Bergen: 99; /Ian Dickson: 42, 58-59, 61, 63, 68; /Gems: 90; /Michael Ochs: 20-21,43; /Eamonn McCabe: 135; /Keith Morris: 24; /Gai Terrell: 91; /David Warner Ellis: 72-73

Retna Pictures Ltd: Steve Double: 127; /Chris Foster: 39; /G. Hanekroot / Sunshine: 45; /Jant Macoska: 15; /Michael Putland: 86, 95; /Tees Tabak /Sunshine:19; /Tolca/Sunshine: 49; /Niels Van Iperen: 124; /Lora Voigt: 8

Rex Features: Jonathan Player: 30; /Steve Callaghan: 114; /Everett Collection: 23, 29, 49, 89, 94, 113; /Herbie Knott: 127; /Ilpo Musto: 41, 111; /Alex Oliveira: 133; /Sipa Press: 52; /Snap: 98, 105

S.I.N.: Peter Anderson: 144

Star File Photo Agency Ltd: Bob Gruen: 51: /Chuck Pulin: 83

Topfoto.co.uk: Lisa Law/Imageworks: 13, 139

Every effort has been made to acknowledge correctly and contact the source and/or copyright holder of each picture and Carlton Books Limited apologises for any unintentional errors or omissions that will be corrected in future editions of this book.

INDEX